HOMES AND SHELTERS FOR BACKYARD BIRDS

John Tyson

Photo Credits:

Ron Austing: *p. 6T; 24; 33 (Painted Bunting); 35; 36; 47 (White-throated Sparrow); 53 (Blue Jay); 54; 58*
Jeff Fishbein: *p. 20; 43B*
Dr. M. Heidenreich: *p. 62*
Kaytee Products, Inc.: *p. 4; 7; 25 (Northern Cardinal); 27*
Larry Kimball: *p. 5 (Mountain Bluebird); 13 (Cactus Wren); 23; 34B; 43T; 45B*
Larry Kimball & Barbara Magnuson: *p. 40*
Peter LaTourrette: *p. 22B; 41 all; 56*
Barbara Magnuson: *p. 1 (Western Bluebird); 6; 12; 22T; 29; 37 all*
G. & C. Merker: *p. 59; 60*
Rafi Reyes: *p. 8; 10B; 39B; 51*
Rob & Ann Simpson: *p. 9 (Highbush Cranberry); 14; 32; 34T; 39T; 46; 52*
Mark Smith: *p. 55*
John Tyson: *p. 3 (wren house); 26; 31; 38; 42; 44; 45T; 57*

Drawings of houses and predator guards by **Suzanne Boehning** *from author's sketches.*

T.F.H. Publications
One TFH Plaza
Third and Union Avenues
Neptune City, NJ 07753

ISBN 0-7938-3576-3

www.tfh.com

CONTENTS

A colorful male Indigo Bunting.

Introduction
A Most Rewarding Experience

Amidst the housing developments, parking lots, and suburban sprawl of our world, wild birds face the pressures of decreasing natural habitat. Fortunately, many humans have begun to recognize the role we can play in protecting and improving what habitat remains. The increasingly popular hobby of attracting and providing for wild birds brings us a deeper understanding of nature and a greater intimacy with the birds we strive to protect.

With the creation of a backyard bird sanctuary, individual homeowners can play an important part in aiding our feathered friends. Regardless of where you live—in the city, suburb, or countryside—

A young male Rose-breasted Grosbeak. Shelter, food, and water will bring in many colorful birds.

the opportunity exists in one form or another on your own property. The birds are out there, and by providing certain basic needs such as shelter, they can be attracted in great numbers. In addition to the fun of planning and developing a backyard project, this hobby provides one of the greatest opportunities to learn more about the birds living around us. It also serves as a peaceful and relaxing pastime that provides remarkable therapy from the pressure and stress of a demanding world.

This book will deal with different types and styles of birdhouses and shelters, as well as proper placement and specific design information. It will shed some light on problems often encountered in providing shelters, and additional tips on construction, maintenance, and landscaping for birds. Most importantly, it will help you have a more rewarding experience with backyard birdwatching.

A House Wren perches on a rustic nesting box, bringing a mouthful of food to young in the nest.

American Robins are not cavity-nesting birds, so they will not build in most nesting boxes. They may occupy nesting shelves, however.

Before putting up a nesting box, take a close look at what your yard has to offer to the birds you want to attract.

Chapter One

HOME
SWEET HOME

Birdhouses serve a very real purpose in a backyard habitat. However, it's important to begin any backyard birdhouse project by first making an initial evaluation of your property. Take a careful look at existing vegetation, natural shelters, food and water sources, as well as the types of birds that frequent your area. Each species of bird has its own specific nesting requirements—some won't even use a birdhouse—so it may be important to provide a variety of houses and shelters.

In order for your efforts to be successful, four necessary environmental elements must be present. Although these aspects of a natural habitat do not necessarily

A gourmet seed mix will help you attract a wide variety of garden birds, from cardinals and finches to woodpeckers. Photo courtesy of Kaytee® Products, Inc.

need to be found within the exact limits of your property, they must be close at hand.

First, a varied food source must be part of the overall plan. The nutritional requirements of wild birds will vary with different species, regions, and at different times of the year. Natural foods, commercial seed mixes, suet, fruit, insects, and nectar all become part of one major variable required for attracting wild birds. Different foods will attract different birds, and a good guide to feeding birds will give information on preferences, seasonal variations, and so forth. With some research and experimentation, you can develop the right combination of seed mixes and food choices that will compliment your bird-housing program.

Don't forget to supply water for your birds. This Carolina Chickadee is drinking from rain on the hanging hook.

Another major requirement is water. The source can be as simple as a faucet dripping into a shallow pan, a birdbath, or a beautifully landscaped bird pond. Depending on the size and type of the water source, other wildlife such as insects, amphibians, reptiles, and mammals will also be attracted.

The third variable for attracting birds is cover. Cover, or shelter, provides protection from predators, wind, snow, sun, and rain. It becomes a place to raise young, retreat, sleep, and rest. Cover can vary in form, including shrubs, brush piles, burrows, live trees, dead trees, building ledges, bridges, rock piles, and man-made birdhouses. The more cover you can offer, the more species diversity you will see develop in your backyard sanctuary.

The final variable is space. All wildlife, including birds, have their own space requirements. These requirements can vary according to the season. In general it is important to keep in mind that every pair of birds will have its own territory to defend. Each species will defend its nesting area from other members of its own kind, preventing other birds from nesting too close. The size of these territories will vary according to species, and for some birds these territories can be quite large.

For example, a pair of Pileated Woodpeckers requires nearly 100 acres of space. A pair of bluebirds may defend almost a full acre of land for nesting rights. The American Robin is often seen hopelessly fighting its own reflection in a glass window or glass door, trying to drive off an unwanted intruder in its territory.

Learning as much as possible about a specific bird's range, behavior, and feeding habits will be helpful in implementing a successful home and shelter program. It's also important to remember that your efforts should not be limited to one season. The four basic needs of wildlife must be provided throughout the year if you are to continue to enjoy the birds' presence.

Many choices in birdseeds, from basic mixes to specialty blends, as well as bells and cakes, are available. Choose what is right for your yard and the birds you wish to attract. Photo courtesy of Kaytee® Products, Inc.

Purple Martin enthusiasts lavish a great deal of attention on their nesting boxes.

Chapter Two

BIRDHOUSE BASICS

How to Make a House a Home

There are two different types of homes that can provide shelter for nesting birds in a backyard habitat. The two are generally categorized as cavity and non-cavity, based on where a bird will naturally nest. A cavity-nesting bird is one that typically nests in the cavity or hole of a dead tree or hollow tree branch; for these birds you could provide a birdhouse, also called a nest box. Non-cavity nesting birds are the birds that typically build their nest on the ledge of a building or in the fork of a tree. With these birds, you could provide an open-fronted nest box or platform for nest building.

Homes for Cavity-Nesting Birds

HELPFUL TIP

The exact dimensions of entrance holes are more important than the dimensions of the actual house.

Many common birds naturally nest in tree cavities and are easy to attract to a backyard and to the shelters provided there. Titmice, chickadees, nuthatches, flickers, bluebirds, swallows, Purple Martins, and many of the woodpeckers are just a few. However, one size does not fit all. Each species of bird should have a birdhouse built specifically for that bird. Simply put, in order to attract a specific bird to a birdhouse, certain dimensional details must be adhered to in the construction process. These specifications will suit a particular species and will prevent unwanted birds from taking up occupancy.

The Tufted Titmouse and its chickadee relatives are classic cavity-nesters.

A wide variety of commercially made birdhouses are available for purchase, often as kits or fully assembled. They can typically be obtained from pet shops, wild bird specialty shops, feed stores, garden centers, or large retail chain stores. Keep in mind that not all manufactured birdhouses are appropriate for nesting. Many serve as wonderful ornamental additions to a garden area, but are not necessarily attractive to birds; many are not even practical for a pair to nest in. In these cases, a nice display, an empty home, and a disgruntled landlord (you!) are usually the end results. Building your own birdhouse allows for a great deal of innovation and creativity, as well as control over the eventual tenants.

HELPFUL TIP

Proper ventilation and drainage are critical in a birdhouse.

BASIC DESIGN AND MATERIALS

All good cavity-nesting birdhouses share some common characteristics, which can then be slightly altered to accommodate most species of cavity-nesting birds. Other than subtle differences in hole size, hole location, and actual box size, the overall construction of the house should follow some general guidelines. With some planning and consideration, you'll have the advantage of building a quality house right from the start, which will result in less frustration for you and greater success with the birds you are trying to attract.

HELPFUL TIP

Remember, the true measurements of a 1x6 board are actually 3/4 x 5 1/2 inches.

Resist any temptations to skimp on materials. Select a type of wood that is natural, and not green or wet, to prevent warping, cracking, and splitting. Natural woods such as redwood, cedar, cypress, white pine, and poplar will work well for a long-lasting birdhouse. Because pressure-treated lumber is chemically preserved with copper arsenate, which can be toxic to birds, it should be avoided. Even exterior plywood can contain

Continued on Page 20

DIMENSIONS FOR BIRDHOUSES

BIRD SPECIES	SIZE OF BOX FLOOR / HEIGHT	ENTRANCE HOLE SIZE	FLOOR TO HOLE HEIGHT	PLACEMENT HEIGHT	BEST LOCATION
House Wren	4 x 4 x 6-8"	1-1 1/4"	4-6"	6-10'	small trees
Bewick's Wren	4 x 4 x 6-8"	1 1/4"	4-6"	6-10'	thickets
Carolina Wren	4 x 4 x 6-8"	1 1/2"	4-6"	6-10'	thickets
Chickadees	4 x 4 x 8-10"	1 1/8"	6-8"	6-15'	woodland
Nuthatches	4 x 4 x 8-10"	1 1/4"	6-8"	12-20'	woodland
Titmice	4 x 4 x 8-10"	1 1/4"	6-8"	6-15'	woodland
Downy Woodpecker	4 x 4 x 8-10"	1 1/4"	6-8"	12-25'	woodland
Hairy Woodpecker	6 x 6 x 15"	1 1/2"	10"	12-20'	woodland
Red-headed Woodpecker	6 x 6 x 12-15"	2"	9-12"	12-20'	woodland
Red-bellied Woodpecker	6 x 6 x 12-15"	2 1/2"	9-12"	12-20'	woodland
Northern flicker	7 x 7 x 16-18"	2 1/2"	14-16"	6-20'	woodland
Bluebirds	5 x 5 x 8"	1 1/2"	6"	3-5'	open pasture
Violet-Green swallow	5 x 5 x 6"	1 1/2"	6-8"	5-8'	semi-open woodland
Tree Swallow	5 x 5 x 6"	1 1/2"	6-8"	5-8'	water/trees
Purple Martin	6 x 6 x 6"	2 1/4"	1"	12-20"	clearing/water
Crested Flycatcher	6 x 6 x 15"	2"	6-8"	8-20'	edge of field
Ash-throated Flycatcher	6 x 6 x 15"	2"	6-8"	8-20'	open woods, wooded stream
Saw - whet Owl	6 x 6 x 10-12"	2 1/2"	8-10"	12-20'	damp woodlands
Screech Owl	8 x 8 x 12-15"	3"	9-12"	10-30'	edge of woods
Barn Owl	10 x 18 x 15-18"	6"	4"	12-18'	open fields
Kestrel (Sparrow Hawk)	8 x 8 x 12-15"	3"	9-12'	10-30'	edge of woods
Wood Duck	10 x 10 x 24"	3"h x 4"w	18-20"	12-40' (trees) 3-5' (water)	mature woods with pond or lake

* floor sizes indicated are interior dimensions

BASIC BIRDHOUSE DESIGN I

MATERIALS LIST:

* one board 1x6x 52 inches long
* sixteen galvanized #6 1 1/2" wood screws
* two 1 3/4" galvanized decking nails
* one 1 1/2" L-screw for latch
* wood glue

PREDATOR GUARD

ASSEMBLY DIRECTIONS:

This house can be built to accommodate an entrance hole or entrance slot. If slot is desired, cut front panel the dimension of an entrance hole that much shorter, i.e., 1 1/4" hole, cut panel 1 1/4" shorter.

1) Measure and mark dimensions on board and cut out one piece at a time to allow for saw cut.
2) Drill four 1/4" ventilation holes on each side.
3) Cut corners of bottom for drainage and ventilation.
4) Cut out a v-notch in bottom of front panel for L-screw latch.
5) Mark and drill holes for screws for attaching sides, roof, and floor.
6) Attach floor to one side using wood screws and wood glue. First apply thin coating of glue to edge of board, then place screws.
7) Next attach back to floor and side using same procedure as above.
8) Assemble last side and finally attach roof flush against back and overhanging on sides and front using glue and wood screws.
9) Drill appropriate size entrance hole for species of bird desired in front panel and predator guard.
10) Using a rasp or chisel, roughen inside of front panel underneath hole to allow for grasping for easier exiting by baby birds.
11) Attach predator guard to front panel.
12) Front panel should be attached to birdhouse with two galvanized nails as hinge joints pivoting from top. Attach L-screw to serve as latch to front bottom.

1X6X52"

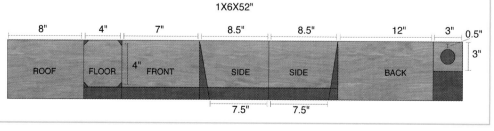

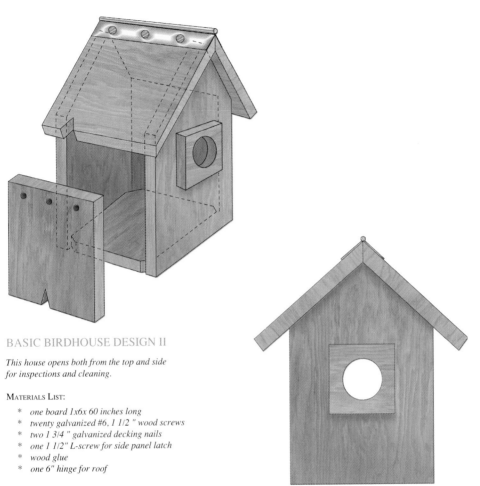

BASIC BIRDHOUSE DESIGN II

*This house opens both from the top and side
for inspections and cleaning.*

MATERIALS LIST:

* one board 1x6x 60 inches long
* twenty galvanized #6, 1 1/2 " wood screws
* two 1 3/4 " galvanized decking nails
* one 1 1/2" L-screw for side panel latch
* wood glue
* one 6" hinge for roof

ASSEMBLY DIRECTIONS:

1) Measure and mark dimensions on board and cut out one piece at a time to allow for saw cut.
2) Drill four 1/4" ventilation holes on each side.
3) Cut corners of bottom for drainage and ventilation.
4) Cut out a v-notch in bottom of side panel for L-screw latch. Also cut v-notch in corner of roof for latch.
5) Mark and drill holes for screws for attaching sides, roof, and floor.
6) Attach floor to one side using wood screws and wood glue. First apply thin coating of glue to edge of board, then place screws.
7) Next attach back to floor using same procedure as above.
8) Drill appropriate size entrance hole for species of bird desired in front panel and predator guard.
9) Using a rasp or chisel, roughen inside of front panel underneath hole to allow for easier grasping for exiting by baby birds.
10) Attach predator guard with four screws to front panel.
11) Attach front panel to birdhouse with wood screws.
12) Assemble last side with two galvanized nails to act as pivot point. Attach L-screw as latch to side bottom.
13) Attach one roof panel with glue and four wood screws flush against back and overhanging on sides and front.
14) Attach hinge to roof panel and finally attach last roof panel with screws to opposite roof panel already on birdhouse.

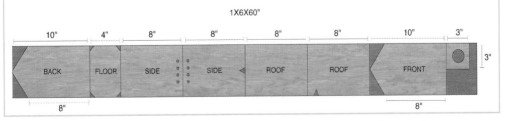

1X6X60"

WREN / CHICKADEE HOUSE

MATERIALS LIST:

* one board 1 x 6 x 48 inches long
* twenty #6 1 1/2 " galvanized wood screws
* wood glue
* cedar shake shingles (optional)

ASSEMBLY DIRECTIONS:

1) Measure and mark dimensions on board and cut out one piece at a time to allow for saw cut.
2) Drill entrance hole in front and predator guard.
3) Roughen inside of front panel with rasp or chisel for grasping by baby birds for easier exit.
4) Drill ventilation holes in floor and sides.
5) Attach predator guard to front using four screws.
6) Attach front and back panel to floor with four wood screws, two on front and two on back.
7) Attach each side with wood screws, four on each side.
8) Screw each roof panel to top of house with four wood screws on each panel.
9) Drill two holes in wood dowel and screw to one roof panel (other roof panel should be used for inspections and cleaning).
10) Add cedar shake shingles or a second layer of roofing for a more rustic look .

1X6X48"

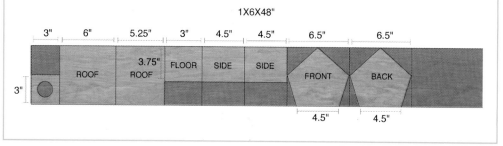

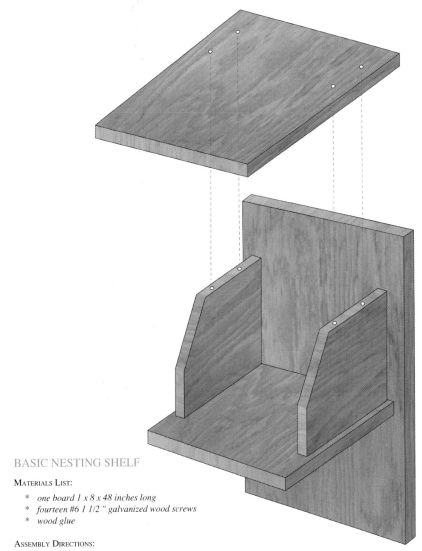

BASIC NESTING SHELF

MATERIALS LIST:

* one board 1 x 8 x 48 inches long
* fourteen #6 1 1/2 " galvanized wood screws
* wood glue

ASSEMBLY DIRECTIONS:

1) Measure and mark dimensions on board and cut out one piece at a time to allow for saw cut.
2) Attach sides to floor with wood glue and four wood screws (two on each side). Inset sides on floor 1/2" on each side.
3) Fasten back to floor and sides using glue and six wood screws.
4) Attach roof to nesting shelf using remaining four wood screws and glue, two on each side.

DIMENSIONS FOR NESTING SHELVES

SPECIES	FLOOR SIZE	HEIGHT OF HOUSE	HEIGHT ABOVE GROUND
Robin	6" x 8"	8"	6' -15'
Song Sparrow	6" x 6"	6"	1' - 3'
Phoebe	6" x 6"	6"	8' -12'
Swallow	6" x 6"	6"	8' -12' (Barn or Cliff)

House Wrens nest in almost any structure with an opening large enough to accommodate their bodies. This simple nesting box is home to a nesting pair.

dangerously high levels of formaldehyde. The inside of the house should always be left untreated; if necessary, any wood that needs to be protected from the elements may be sealed on the outside. The wood selected should be a minimum of 3/4-inch to 1-inch thick. A thicker wood, in comparison to metal, ceramic, or a thinner wood, is a much better insulator from heat and cold.

CONSTRUCTION 101

A birdhouse should include some basic elements. The top of the birdhouse should be constructed to include a slightly sloping roof that extends several inches out beyond the front, providing a shaded entrance and protection from wind-driven rains. A recessed floor with drainage holes will aid in controlling the dampness, cleanliness, and ventilation of the house. Additional $1/4$-inch ventilation holes or slots should be located just under the roofline.

Do not include a perch on the outside of the house; this will discourage House Sparrows and European Starlings, which are considered pests by many birdwatchers and landlords, from taking occupancy. The absence of perches will also help to deter predators from taking a foothold onto the front of the house. Cavity-nesting birds do not need a perch to gain access to the inside of the house and the absence of one will help in establishing, the type of bird you are interested in. However, the wood on the inside of the house below the entrance can be grooved or fitted with wire mesh to give baby birds something to grab on to when leaving the nesting box.

To further prevent predators from entering, the entrance hole should be fitted with an additional $3/4$-inch thick square piece of wood around the outside of the hole (drill a hole through this piece to match the hole of the nest box). The added thickness of the predator guard will help prevent the paws of cats or raccoons from being able to reach down from the outside and into the cavity of the house.

Several methods are commonly used for protecting the outside of the birdhouse from inclement weather. Cypress, redwood, and cedar woods are considered ideal materials; because of their natural weather-resistant

HELPFUL TIP
Use galvanized wood screws rather the glue, staples, or nails to assemble a birdhouse.

HELPFUL TIP
Do not use pressure-treated lumber since it can be lethal to birds.

tendencies they do not need any chemical preservatives. However, if pine and plywood are used they may be treated to sustain the longer life of the wood. The outside of the box may be sealed with a stain or with a lead-free water-based paint; another option is to apply several coats of linseed oil. Be certain that only the outside is sealed, and do not apply a sealant around the entrance hole or inside the house. Bright or ornamental colors serve no purpose for birds, which prefer light and natural colors such as grays, browns, and greens. These colors reflect heat and sunlight much better and are less conspicuous to predators. Be aware that research has shown that applying a sealant on the birdhouses will sometimes deter the use of the house for a longer time period than if no sealant was used.

The best quality birdhouses are held together with more than staples and glue. When assembling the house, use wood glue at the non-moving joints and stainless steel or galvanized wood screws to hold the pieces together. Galvanized nails may also be used, but should be used minimally and only where screws are not possible. A hinged side and/or rooftop is recommended for ease of cleaning and inspections.

The dimensional chart is formulated only as a guideline for basic construction for different species. Keep in mind that the entrance hole dimension is extremely critical. Being off by only $1/8$ inch can allow the wrong birds to gain access or prohibit the right birds from getting in. However, for most amateur woodworkers, differences in the other dimensions—if the birdhouse is slightly narrower and 2 inches taller than a given plan, for example—may not make a great deal of difference. In nature, a natural

NESTING MATERIALS

To set up housekeeping in a nest box or shelter, birds require nesting materials, which will vary from species to species. Natural nests are usually constructed from materials such as moss, dried and green grasses, stems, pieces of bark, feathers, pine needles, spider webs, leaves, and mud. However, a number of studies into the nesting habits of birds have shown that birds will in many instances use whatever materials are accessible. Wren nests have been known to contain everything from the traditional small twigs to nails, pins, and paper clips. Robins, swallows, and songbirds may pick up small white feathers from a pair of swans in a nearby pond or wool fragments from the flock of sheep up the road.

Homeowners can make the chore of gathering materials easier. Yarn, pieces of string, feathers, horse hair, ribbon, twine, clothes dryer lint, and pet fur can be offered in a small wire suet basket and hung from a tree; the same basket can be used after the breeding season for suet. Mesh bags that oranges and potatoes come in also make good receptacles. Cut the material pieces into lengths of 6 inches or less to prevent any unwanted or unforeseen tragedies such as strangulation and broken wings, feet, and toes; lengths longer than 6 inches can easily become entangled around the bird and caught on natural objects such as tree branches. Because not all birds nest in the spring and several species have more than one brood, it is a good idea to keep nesting materials available from April through August. Many Cedar Waxwings and finches will not nest until late summer and will also indulge in an offering of nesting materials.

Backyard birdwatchers may also choose to keep a supply of mud available for robins and Barn and Cliff Swallows, which will seek out mud sources for their nest building. No robin nest is complete without mud, and swallow colonies use a great deal of it. An isolated area of a garden or flowerbed works well for this and will be easily utilized by the birds and easily monitored by you.

21

cavity in a hollow tree is never the exacting dimensions illustrated on a chart. The important point is that the house has adequate room for the parent birds and brood. Your finished product should be close to the appropriate size, sturdy, weather-resistant, easily maintained, and easily inspected.

Homes for Non-cavity-nesting Birds

Black Phoebes usually build a nest in a tight crevice under a bridge or a barn roof; they also will use nesting shelves.

Open-fronted nesting boxes are designed for birds that do not nest in natural tree cavities or birdhouses but on ledges or tree branches. An open-fronted nest box, also called a nesting shelf, is most likely to be used by robins, swallows, Song Sparrows, and phoebes. These structures are basically a platform without a front. Some styles are also designed without sides, and sometimes without a roof, depending on the species for which it is built. The design you decide upon should be partially determined by where the shelf will be located and by how much protection it receives from the weather.

CONSTRUCTION 101

A nesting shelf is inexpensive and easy to make. It should be made of the same quality lumber and materials as a birdhouse. The only difference with these structures is that they should not be treated on the outside, but left as natural wood. For the robins, thrushes, Song Sparrows, and phoebes, include a sloped roof in the actual design of the platform.

A secluded and partially hidden nesting area is generally most accepted by these species. Try to position the shelf in a location that is obstructed from view with branches or vegetation of some type, such as vine arbors or shrubbery. Depending on the species of bird, 3 to 15 feet above the ground is an appropriate height. The nesting shelf table gives construction dimensions and height suggestions for specific birds.

Song Sparrows may be the most familiar backyard sparrows in the summer. They often will accept nesting shelves in protected areas.

Maintenance

For most birds, clean, empty houses are more attractive for nesting than are those containing an old nest; some birds won't even consider a box that contains nesting leftovers from the previous tenants. Once a pair of birds has raised a clutch and the birds have fledged, the box can be opened and the old nest discarded. Always be certain that the nest is truly abandoned and not newly built. If the possibility exists that the

HELPFUL TIP
Bluebird houses located less than 4 feet above the ground will usually discourage English sparrows from nesting.

birdhouse will be used again during the same nesting season, it should simply be emptied and swept clean. Do not wash out the box with diluted solutions of bleach or other products, which can be toxic to birds.

Once the nest box or shelf is cleaned, chances are good it will become reoccupied. Many wild birds will raise two to three broods each season. Because some pairs will automatically select another site, a cleaned nest box will be ready for the next pair to move in.

Violet-green Swallows commonly occupy bluebird houses in the western states, much as do Tree Swallows in the East.

After the nesting season is over, the inside should be disinfected for lice, mites, and other pests. A 1% rotenone powder or a pyrethrin-based insecticide can safely be used for this purpose. Both of these products can be applied inside the house and will quickly destroy any parasites occupying the inside cracks and corners. None of these chemicals will be harmful to birds if applied in the fall after the nesting season.

HELPFUL TIP
Be sure to build a predator guard to fit over the outside of the entrance hole to further deter predator paws.

Fall is also a good time to make structural repairs on any nest boxes, shelves, or poles. Loose nails, screws, and hinges should be repaired in late fall or early winter so you have time to get the houses back into place before the early migratory birds return.

Bird shelters can be left out during the winter months or brought in out of the harsh weather. If you decide to leave them out, it is a good idea to cover the opening to keep out mice and squirrels. The white-footed deer mouse is a notorious birdhouse occupant. In addition, many squirrel species such as flying squirrels, gray squirrels, and red squirrels love to use boxes erected for Screech Owls, flickers, and other woodpeckers during the colder winter months. If given the chance, many squirrels will also damage and enlarge the entrance holes on nest boxes. You can either choose to let them use the box as a winter shelter and remove them in the spring or close off the hole in the fall before they attempt to set up house.

HELPFUL TIP
Natural colors are better for bird houses, except for the Purple Martin house, which should always be white.

In the South, Carolina Wrens will nest in boxes with suitable openings. For best luck, also provide a birdbath.

Chapter Three

SUCCESS
WITH SHELTERS

Birdhouses should be installed early in the spring or late in winter, depending on the region you live in. Most importantly, houses need to be in place before the migrating birds arrive and well before the onset of the breeding season. Many birds will establish their territories before the breeding season actually begins, so it is important to be prepared before their arrival.

Keep in mind that your yard and the surrounding properties probably all offer slightly different habitats for birds. Take note of the habitat next door as well as your own. Your neighbor's garden or shrubbery may be conducive for birds and allow for the proper

Placement of the nesting box is important. Hanging boxes must be placed where the wind and rain will not cause problems for the birds within, and also where the sun will not bake the young.

placement of a birdhouse along the property line. When placing a birdhouse, it is important to remember that not all birds nest in the same area. Even the best-planned and best-made birdhouse may never be used if the proper habitat is not present for a particular bird. Some birds are not as particular as others; although not every homeowner has habitat for Wood Ducks, woodpeckers, Purple Martins, or owls, most can attract a variety of songbirds, including titmice, chickadees, and robins.

Factors to consider when actually determining the site for the box should include the direction the box will face and the amount of cover it will offer the bird. A birdhouse should not face directly into prevailing winds and strong rains that could potentially enter the box and soak the interior. A partially sunny location, as opposed to dense shade, facing southeast to northeast, is ideal. However, in extremely hot regions a nest box facing directly south could easily overheat and prove detrimental to the chicks. Try to determine the location of the birdhouse before any foliage begins to fall so you can easily identify where the heavily shaded areas are.

Many birds prefer open nesting areas where they have a good view of the nest from all directions. Others will require the house to be located in an area that offers protection and privacy. Either way, there should be a clear path to the entrance hole of the house. Generally, secluded spots away from constant human activity work well. However, these secluded spots may hold other dangers. Be sure the area does not provide a hidden location for cats to sit, watch, and become potential predators of the parents as they fly to and from the nest.

You should also avoid placing the house near birdfeeders or feeding stations. Install the house where the birds will have privacy, away from continual birdfeeding and human activity.

Birdhouses that are attached to poles are generally more protected from predators than those that hang from branches or that attach directly to a tree trunk. Poles are considerably more difficult for predators to climb than are trees, especially if you use smooth PVC pipe to hamper any climbing tendencies. Squirrel

Red-headed Woodpeckers often nest in artificial nests made from chunks of natural branches and placed in a suitably wooded area.

guards or baffles, such as those that are often used for birdfeeders, will also give added protection from climbing predators when fastened to the pole under the house. Be sure to place the pole far enough away from trees or buildings that might become jumping or launching areas for cats or squirrels. Hanging the birdhouse from a chain under an eave or from a tree branch also works.

Whatever method you decide to use, be sure the house is securely attached. The weight of an adult raccoon or a gust of strong wind can easily dislodge a birdhouse that is not securely anchored and assembled. It can be quite disheartening to get up in the morning and find your bluebird house on the ground with tiny paw prints all over it. The extra effort of properly placing your birdhouses from the start will be well worth it in the long run.

SUCCESS WITH WRENS

Several nest boxes of the same type can be helpful in settling a wren pair into your backyard. The male wren has been known to build as many as a dozen nests in the spring. He then takes the female around to show her his handiwork, from which she selects the house of her liking where the eggs will later be laid. By providing several birdhouses for wrens, your chances are much improved that a pair of wrens will take up residency in your backyard bird sanctuary.

How Many Birdhouses?

In lots of an acre or less, erecting more than one birdhouse for each species can be fruitless. Other than giving the bird an opportunity to choose from more than one nest, or the possibility of having another nest available after the first clutch is raised, the box will probably remain empty. Because nesting birds will defend their territory, a nesting pair is not likely to allow another pair of the same species to nest too closely. One exception is the colony-type birds such as the swallows and martins, which will nest together in large groups.

If you would like to put up several birdhouses in your yard, try to erect different birdhouses for different species of birds and keep them as far apart as possible. Generally, a distance of 25 feet works well.

Checking the Birdhouse

Once a breeding pair has established residency and has begun nest-building, many people choose to make periodic inspections of the nest boxes. However, it's important that these inspections be brief and cause little or no disruption to the birds.

A hinged side wall or front wall is handy for cleaning, but actual nest inspections are best made from the top of the house. After approaching the birdhouse, lightly tap on the sides to allow the occupants to know of your presence. Slowly lift the top, make a quick visual inspection for parasites or

Though somewhat different in their preferences from the more common Eastern and Western Bluebirds, the blue-breasted Mountain Bluebird also accepts nest boxes when properly placed at the edges of open meadows and fields.

29

NESTING SPECIFICATIONS OF SOME FAMILIAR BIRDS

SPECIES	NESTING PREFERENCE	NESTING MATERIAL	NUMBER EGGS (BROODS)	COLOR OF EGGS
House Wren	cavity	twigs, grass, misc. items	6-7 (2-3)	white w/brown spots
Tufted Titmouse	cavity	grasses	4-8 (1-2)	white w/brown specks
Black-capped Chickadee	cavity	wood chips	6-8 (1-2)	white w/red/brown specks
Carolina Wren	cavity	grasses, leaves, weeds	4-8 (2-3)	creamy white w/brown
Eastern Bluebird	cavity	grasses	3-5 (2-3)	light blue
Northern Flicker	cavity	wood chips	7-9 (1-2)	white
Screech Owl	cavity	wood chips	3-5 (1)	white
American Robin	forks of trees/ nesting shelf	grasses & mud	4 (2-3)	pastel blue
Phoebe	ledges, nesting shelf	mud, grass, feathers	3-6 (2)	white
White-Breasted Nuthatch	cavity	twigs, grass, bark strips	5-10 (1-2)	white w/lavender & brown specks
Tree Swallow	cavity	grasses, feathers	4-6 (1-2)	white
Purple Martin	cavity	grasses	4-6 (1)	white
Red-headed Woodpecker	cavity	wood chips	4-5 (1-2)	white
Red-bellied Woodpecker	cavity	wood chips	3-8 (1-3)	white
Wood Duck	cavity	wood chips	9-12 (1-2)	whitish tan
Barn Swallow	building ledges, nesting shelf	mud & feathers	3-5 (2-3)	white w/reddish brown specks
Great Crested Flycatcher	cavity	twigs, grasses, lined with shiny material	5-6 (1)	milky white with brown blotches
Violet-green Swallow	cavity	weeds, stems, grasses	4-6 (1-2)	white
Downy Woodpecker	cavity	wood chips	4-5 (1)	white
Hairy Woodpecker	cavity	wood chips	3-6 (1)	white
Bewick's Wren	cavity	grasses, leaves, weeds	5-7 (2)	white w/brown spots
Mountain Bluebird	cavity	grasses	4-6 (2-3)	pale blue
Western Bluebird	cavity	grasses	5-8 (2-3)	pale blue
American Kestrel	cavity	wood chips	4-5 (1)	pinkish w/dark spots
Red-breasted Nuthatch	cavity	grasses & bark strips	5-7 (1-2)	white w/brown specks
Cliff Swallow	ledges or nesting shelf	mud & grass	3-6 (1-3)	white w/brown blotches
Carolina Chickadee	cavity	grasses, plant stems, feathers	6-8 (1-2)	white w/reddish brown spots
Mountain Chickadee	cavity	wood chips & feathers	7-9 (1-2)	white
Mourning Dove	shrub or tree fork/ nesting shelf	loose twigs	2 (2-3)	white
Plain Titmouse	cavity	moss, grasses	6-8 (1-2)	white w/brown spots
Ash-throated Flycatcher	cavity	stems, rootlets, chips of manure	4-5 (1)	white w/dark spots
Pygmy Nuthatch	cavity	bark, pine cone scales, hair	4-9 (1)	white w/dark spots

predators, then close the top and leave the nest undisturbed. If the house has chicks in it, opening it from a hinged side or front can sometimes result in the babies hopping out. If this happens, gently pick them up and quickly put them back in the box. Don't worry about the parents rejecting them; it is a myth that birds can smell human scent on the babies and will not take them back.

One of the most important things you can do when making nest inspections is to record your findings. Nesting box records are an important way of monitoring the success of your project. By keeping records, you can determine when and where any problems such as predation began and what types of changes were successful.

Data collection can actually begin from the first observed nesting activity after the nest box is installed. When more than one house is being observed, it is a good idea to assign a number to the birdhouse and write the number somewhere on the house. Record information such as when the pair first arrived, when nest -building began, and what types of materials were included in the nest. Also record when the first egg was laid, how many eggs were laid, and when the brood hatched and fledged from the nest.

CONSERVATION COUNTS

In addition to serving your monitoring needs, the nesting records you keep can be extremely important for field research that is being conducted and collected by several ornithological organizations

Homemade nesting boxes are designed to be opened for cleaning, but purchased boxes may lack any way of opening. You must be able to open the box for regular cleaning.

Eastern Bluebirds have responded very well to bluebird trails maintained by volunteer groups.

Chapter Four

LANDLORDING TIPS

Bluebirds

The beautiful bluebird is a sought-after resident of many backyard birders. North America has three species of bluebirds: the Western Bluebird, the Eastern Bluebird, and the Mountain Bluebird. All three will use nest boxes.

A vibrant sky blue color and reddish breast (in the Eastern and Western), along with a beautiful warbling song, have made the birds a perennial favorites. The male bluebird is so intensely colored that he is quickly identified by even the beginning birdwatcher. A bluebird's temperament is quite trusting and friendly when approached with patience and kindness, and some may even seem to recognize their landlords.

Though they have once again become relatively common in some areas, there still is a thrill that comes from seeing Eastern Bluebirds in the field.

At one time, bluebird populations were rapidly declining because of the widespread destruction of their habitat. In fact, many people still have never seen one of these cherished birds in the wild. However, bluebird nesting box programs have become extremely widespread and successful, despite ongoing competition and predation from European Starlings, House Sparrows, and raccoons.

If you live in an area that borders open grassy fields, you will most likely be able to attract bluebirds. They seem to prefer a nest box in the open—with a view of predators—versus a concealed or partially hidden box in an area of thick vegetation. The natural nesting site of bluebirds is often in a woodpecker hole in a rotted tree, a hollow apple tree, or the top of the rotted portion of a fence post. The preferred location is along the edge of a farm field, orchard, or pasture with scattered trees and grasses. These areas provide the bluebird with an abundant supply of insects, which constitute about 90 percent of its summertime diet. Keeping this in mind, select an area that is open in every direction. Mounting the birdhouse less than 5 feet above the ground will discourage sparrows from nesting because they prefer to be much higher than this. Try to keep multiple bluebird houses at least 100 yards apart.

Chickadees, Titmice, and Nuthatches

There are several species of chickadees, titmice, and nuthatches found throughout the United States, all which are cavity-nesting birds. If you have a wooded lot, chances are that these birds may take notice of your birdhouse. All three groups occupy the same woodland type habitat and will regularly visit a feeder.

Chickadees, nuthatches, and titmice all nest in natural tree cavities. The competition for natural nesting sites can be quite keen between them and red squirrels, gray squirrels, and flying squirrels. Supplying nest boxes for these birds can be helpful in diminishing the intense competition between these birds and mammals for natural nesting space.

One species of chickadee or another is found in backyards in every part of the country. This is the Mountain Chickadee of the Rockies.

A basic birdhouse design with the appropriate hole size and dimensions will work well for these species. They prefer a rustic, unfinished look to a decoratively painted house. Rough cedar, weathered wood, and a cedar shingles covered with bark make an attractive house. The Black-capped Chickadee and the Carolina Chickadee occupy similar habitats; houses hung or mounted at eye level will prove to be quite successful with them. Titmice, such as the Tufted Titmouse and the Plain Titmouse, will nest anywhere from 6 to 15 feet above the ground, whereas nuthatch species will require a nest from 12 to 20 feet or higher. Because these birds are woodland birds, the boxes for these species can be located in a partially shaded area along a wooded border, mounted in a tree or on a post for protection from climbing predators such as the raccoon.

Chickadees, nuthatches, and titmice are all charming birds that show little fear of humans and may become quite tame.

> ## WOOD CHIP ALERT
>
> Red cedar wood chips should not be provided as nesting material because of the harmful effect that they have on birds. Choose other wood chips, shavings, and materials instead.

Woodpeckers and Flickers

Several species of woodpeckers are regular visitors to backyards, and some can be persuaded to use a nesting box. Woodpeckers such as the Red-headed, Downy, and Hairy are regulars at the feeder, but are not as easy to entice to a nesting box. The greatest success is likely to be experienced with the Red-bellied Woodpecker and the Northern Flicker. Again, the appropriate size house should be used. Woodpeckers, which are also woodland-type birds, require rustic-looking houses mounted 12 to 20 feet up or higher. It is also recommended to fill the bottom of the house with moist soil and wood shavings or chips as bedding; this will serve to replicate the wood chips and rotted wood pieces that result in a natural home during the excavation process. Flickers will generally not nest in an artificial box without at least 2 inches of material added to the bottom.

A male Yellow-bellied Sapsucker at its nest. Woodpeckers generally accept only nests that are almost natural in appearance and structure.

Purple Martins

The ever-popular Purple Martin is a swallow-type colony bird with very specific housing requirements. A Purple Martin house basically consists of one unit with as few 8 to 36 or more individual compartments mounted on a long pole. The entire unit is then raised 12 to 20 feet above the ground in an appropriate location.

Although there are many styles of Purple Martin apartment houses to choose from, there are basically three different types: aluminum, wooden, and gourd. Each has its own advantages and disadvantages. The aluminum houses are much easier to get up in the air than the heavy wooden ones, yet they are flimsier and provide less insulating properties. The aluminum variety may

also lack the latest in design from current research as far as entry holes and compartment sizes.

Before deciding on a specific house, be sure to determine what type of pole system you are going to use to raise and lower the unit. Choose one that allows you to make periodic inspections and take care of routine maintenance on the birdhouse unit itself. Raising and lowering the martin house should be easily accomplished and more of a concern to a landlord than what the house looks like.

ADULT

The wooden houses, although much heavier, are sturdier and can be constructed with a pulley system to allow inspections and maintenance.

Carefully analyze the house or the plans you are interested in. Be certain that the dimensions and specifications are correct. Some of the most resent research shows that martins will generally accept an entrance hole as small as $1^3/_4$ up to $2^1/_2$ inches in diameter. Most plans will properly use a 2-/ or $2^1/_4$-inch hole. The housing cavity should be a minimum size of 6 by 6 inches. Some of the more recently designed houses include cavity entrances that repel starlings and deeper compartments to help protect eggs; others have eliminated unnecessary porches and railings.

Martins can also be enticed to nest in large gourds, which can be purchased or grown right in your own backyard. Gourds are colorful and their shapes can add a touch of amusement and rustic charm. The birthhouse or large bottle-type variety of gourd plant will produce more than enough martin homes for the average backyard. A 2-inch entrance hole should be drilled in the side of the gourd about 1 inch up from the base; the dried seeds and fiber material should then be removed. Several $1/4$-inch holes should be drilled near the bottom of the gourd to help provide additional

NESTLING

ventilation and drainage, and a hook can be attached to the top of the gourd for hanging. Several guards can be strung up on lines and retrieved by a pulley system; they can also be hung directly underneath an already existing martin house. Gourds are lightweight, easily replaced, and they provide good ventilation. Their tendency to sway in the wind also helps discourage sparrows and starlings from taking up residency.

ARTIFICIAL GOURD HOUSES

There are more than one million martin houses in the United States; unfortunately, for a number of reasons, a very low percentage of these ever attract or are successful at housing Purple Martins. Your chances will greatly improve if you keep a few rules in mind.

- Good Purple Martin habitat must be available. First, check in a field guide to see that your property is located within the martins' summer nesting range. Simply put, if you are not within their migratory range, you won't get martins. There must also be good open feeding habitat nearby. Martins will travel one to two miles to feed, but usually not farther. A natural water source such as a pond, lake, or river definitely adds appeal but is not a requirement.

LOWERING A HOUSE

- The actual location of the unit is extremely important. Mount the house in a clearing with at least a 40-foot diameter, free from all obstacles including trees and vegetation. It should also be at least 100 feet from human activity such as a house or building. Be certain that there are no wires attached to the martin house or too close to it for squirrels to gain access. The base of the martin house and pole should be kept free and clear from any bushy vegetation that would attract snakes or other predators.

- Check any plans or manufactured houses for correct specifications. They are not all the same.

- Research has shown that martins prefer houses that are painted white. White reflects the summer sun, and bird losses due to heat are fewer. In addition, white enhances the dark entrance hole for martins searching for housing in the spring. Cedar, redwood, and even gourd houses should be painted white to increase your chances of success.

Swallows

Several species of swallows can be successfully attracted to artificial nest boxes. These are popular birds with many homeowners because their diet is based predominately on insects. Barn Swallows, Tree Swallows, Violet-green Swallows, and Purple Martins are all colony-type birds.

A natural swallow nest is usually built out of mud, feathers, straw, and grasses. Because mud is the main source of nesting material during the breeding season, provide birds with a good supply of it from the corner of the garden. Swallows are wonderful little birds to watch in flight, and their tranquil nature adds a touch of peacefulness to a backyard.

Barn Swallows commonly nest under eaves and other tight, protected high places.

The Tree Swallow will readily accept a nest box with an entrance hole. Although they seem to prefer boxes attached to dead trees, they often take up residency in bluebird houses mounted to a pole. Because Tree Swallows live in colonies, they can be attracted to several houses spaced 7 to 8 feet apart. Water and woods appear to be key ingredients; ideal locations are the edges of fields and along ponds, lakes, or streams.

Though the opening for the box is obviously too large, Tree Swallows have chosen to construct their nest here. These swallows may become pests if you want bluebirds in your boxes.

The Violet-green Swallow will also use a cavity birdhouse. Preferred placement areas are along the edges of fields and woods in semi-open areas. Large trees make the best mounting posts.

Not all of the swallow family birds will nest in nest boxes. The Barn and Cliff Swallows, whose nests typically are located inside barns, under bridges, or under building eaves, should be provided with a shelf or platform for nesting. Consequently, the shelf needs to be mounted up against the wall under an overhang of some sort. The construction process is rather simple. Build a nesting shelf as you would for the robins and phoebes, but omit any type of roof. The overhang from the roof of the building will provide necessary shelter from the sun and rain.

Wrens

The House Wren, Carolina Wren, and Bewick's Wren are energetic, somewhat drab birds, but with big personalities and plenty of charm, they are favorites of backyard birders. Although temperament and size vary among species, the three will readily accept backyard houses.

Seeing House Wrens feeding their young is enjoyable, but sometimes there can be just too many nesting wrens in a yard.

Wrens have arrived in spring when you hear the male attempting to attract a female with his continuous joyous song. You may also start to find small piles of sticks in birdhouses, flower pots, the pockets of clothes on the clothesline, or in tin cans, mailboxes, and other unusual places. Wrens are not picky about where they build their nests; if it is a hole they can fit into, it is an appropriate place to build.

The House Wren is known to be more territorial than its close cousins. They will generally claim an area as large as a quarter of an acre and have been known to aggressively attack and ward off other bird intruders, large or small. Even the safety of other nesting species can be at risk if located within the chosen territory of a pair of wrens. House Wrens have been known to invade existing nests within their selected territory and destroy eggs, kill baby birds, and chase off adults. Those with a limited amount of property who also hope to attract other songbirds should carefully consider whether they should extend an invitation to wrens.

The basic cavity-style birdhouse is easily accepted by wrens. The entrance hole should be no larger than 1 $^1/_4$ inch in diameter to keep out

House Sparrows and predators. Because wrens use a lot of small sticks and twigs for nesting material, a birdhouse with a slot for an entrance versus a hole works well. The slot should measure no more than 1 $^1/_4$ inches high and several inches wide. The male will build several nests for the female to choose from, so it is a good idea to put out several boxes for these birds. The birdhouse can be hung from a tree branch in an area that provides some additional shelter and cover. The resulting swaying motion does not bother the wrens, but it will further help deter other birds and predators. Wrens will nest twice each summer. After that they retreat into the dense underbrush and deep woods and are very seldom seen for the remainder of the summer months.

Even though they can be pests, it is illegal to destroy the nests of House Wrens or to disturb their movements.

Flycatchers

Woodland is the preferred habitat choice of the Great Crested and Ash-throated flycatchers. When possible, abandoned woodpecker holes are usually chosen as the natural nesting sites of these birds. However, birdhouses located near a stream and an open wooded area will have the best chance of attracting these insect-loving creatures. The nest box should be constructed with the appropriate hole size, with the entrance hole 12 to no more than 18 inches above the floor. To be most effective, the box should then be mounted approximately 10 feet above the ground.

Ash-throated Flycatchers nest in holes in posts and in old woodpecker holes in nature, and they will accept similar cavities in western yards.

Data taken from nest studies of the Great Crested Flycatcher have shown that the birds use bits of snake skin in lining their nests. In today's suburban backyards and woodlands, bits of shiny material such as cellophane, wax paper, and onion skins seem to satisfy their need for an attractive nest. The Ash-throated Flycatcher's nest consists of some unusual items as well, such as bits of manure, small roots, and hair. Both nests will also contain the typical pieces of grasses, stems, and twigs.

41

Robins and Phoebes

For many, the American Robin is recognized as the forerunner of spring. They are easily attracted to large well-groomed grassy yards with ample supplies of earthworms, which comprise a major portion of their diet.

Typically, they will choose a nesting site such as in the fork of a tree or bush or on a horizontal ledge of a building or house. They have also been known to choose nesting sites in rather unusual areas such as hanging flower baskets or on top of unused birdhouses.

Phoebes are small, gentle birds known to nest under the eaves of porches and on the joists of garages, barns, and other buildings in suburban backyards. They also like to nest near water and under bridges, along wooded ravines, and under the upturned roots of fallen trees.

Cover is extremely important for successfully attracting nesting robins and phoebes. A nesting shelf or open-fronted birdhouse should be placed in an area that is partially secluded by vegetation, protected from predators, and placed approximately 6 to 12 feet above the ground. The shelf should be built to proper specifications and include a sloped roof. As with an enclosed birdhouse, the bottom should have $1/4$-inch drainage holes. Use the same quality lumber and materials as you use for the nest boxes, but leave the nesting shelf untreated with stains or paint.

The mud-edged nests of American Robins are a common sight in backyard trees, but only rarely do these birds accept nesting shelves unless cover and a birdbath also are supplied.

Water is also a major draw for both birds. Something as simple as a birdbath or a pan of water will attract robins, which are noted for their vigorous bathing displays. Moving water seems to create even more of an attraction for these birds. Because both use a lot of mud in nest construction, offer an ample supply in a garden area or in a small flat pan.

Nesting materials of string, straw, and yarn will also enhance the possibilities of robins and phoebes nesting in your yard and will add to the fun of watching the nest-building process.

House Sparrows and European Starlings

Many backyard birders and landlords find that they must contend with House Sparrows and European Starlings, non-native but prevalent birds that are considered the greatest competition for cavity-style birdhouses. Much research has gone into entrance hole sizes, shapes of entrance holes, location and positioning of birdhouses, and methods used to discourage these birds from nesting. However, they are both very persistent nest- builders and will usually nest in anything they can fit into.

The untidy nests of House Sparrows are a major nuisance in many yards. These birds are not protected by law, so their nests can be destroyed if you wish.

Some common methods of preventing these pests from invading your backyard sanctuary include using hanging feeders that sway and not providing favored foods such as cracked corn. Also, be certain that your birdhouses are built to specifications and, if necessary, deter them from becoming established in houses meant for other birds by pulling out nesting materials as they are deposited.

Owls and Kestrels

Owls do not typically construct their own nests. Species such as the Great Horned Owl and the Long-eared Owl generally nest in abandoned crow or squirrel nests. Barn Owls will usually nest in farmland areas in places such as silos, barn rafters, and church steeples; they are also attracted to golf courses, fields, and open meadows where they feed on rodents such as rats, mice, and meadow voles. They can be enticed to nest in a cavity-type birdhouse mounted on a pole 15 to 20 feet above the ground or to the side of a building. Two inches of wood chips should be added to the bottom of the house for bedding.

Screech owls often accept secluded nest boxes with relatively large openings. These predators seldom pursue backyard birds.

Other owls such as the Saw-whet will nest in abandoned flicker nests and Pileated Woodpecker nests. They too will accept cavity-style birdhouses. Preferred locations are damp, mature deciduous forests. As with the Barn Owl, position the house 15 to 20 feet up in a mature tree along the forest edge.

In a suburban neighborhood, the outside edges of wooded areas are preferred locations for the screech owl and American Kestrel. They both typically nest in abandoned woodpecker holes. When given the opportunity, however, each species will nest in a wooden nest box, often competing for the same nesting sites. Not only are the habitat and nesting requirements very similar for these birds, their diets are also quite identical. They both eat grasshoppers, crickets, other insects, and mice. The biggest difference in their habits is that the American Kestrel is active during the day and the screech owl is nocturnal.

Kestrels, formerly called Sparrow Hawks, feed mostly on grasshoppers and other large insects and are cavity-nesters. Lucky indeed is the owner who attracts kessies to a nesting box.

Nesting boxes for screech owls and American Kestrels should be built to the appropriate dimensions and mounted 12 to 15 feet above the ground. Ideally, these boxes can be fastened directly to the main trunk of the tree. Wetlands and neglected orchards are excellent locations for the screech owl, and isolated trees along the edges of wooded areas are best for the American Kestrel. Place 2 inches of pine shavings or wood chips into the bottom of the nest box for bedding. screech owl nest boxes should be cleaned out after the young have fledged. Doing so may encourage the American Kestrel to take up residency in the same nest box shortly thereafter.

Wood Ducks

If you have property that contains a shallow wooded stream or pond surrounded by a mature woodland, you can probably attract Wood Ducks. Woodies are cavity-nesting birds that usually require a mature forest and wetland area. Their natural nests are made in tree cavities constructed by gray squirrels or Pileated Woodpeckers, or where decay has removed enough heartwood to form a natural cavity.

Lack of natural nesting sites has motivated many to participate in successful Wood Duck nesting box programs. Woodie populations have made a significant comeback in the past 20 years because of these popular programs implemented by state agencies, county organizations, and private landowners.

The Wood Duck nest box should be well constructed and securely fastened to prevent raccoons, their main predator, from entering or destroying the box. The inside front of the box should be lined with $1/4$-inch wire mesh so the ducklings can easily climb out when ready to leave the box. Several inches of pine or wood chips inside the box for bedding provides an attractive setup for woodies.

A Wood Duck nest box can either be attached to the main trunk of a tree 10 to 20 feet above the ground or mounted to a pole 6 to 8 feet above the water surface. Note that boxes attached to trees are more susceptible to predators and to other animals such as fox squirrels that may attempt to take up residency in the box. When tree mounted, try to have a clear path to the water's edge, free from obstacles such as buildings, streets, or

Wood Duck nesting boxes commonly have oval openings and are sturdily built to deter raccoons and other predators. In many areas a wide, conical predator guard is necessary to keep out snakes.

woven wire fences. Upon hatching, the mother Wood Duck calls and coaxes the young from the box and immediately leads them to the nearest water source.

Nest boxes mounted on poles in the water offer a little more protection from climbing predators and other animals taking up occupancy. The pole should be fitted with a guard or sleeve to prevent climbing predators and snakes from entering the box.

Once threatened by hunting and the feather trade, the Wood Duck has returned in numbers to the eastern U.S., in part due to the many nesting boxes provided in suitable areas by conservation groups.

Almost anything can be used to make a nesting box, but good-quaility untreated wood still is best.

Chapter Five

ALTERNATIVE SHELTERS

Roosting Boxes

Another type of shelter you can make for birds is a roosting box. Roosting boxes are often used as a place of refuge on cold winter nights to sleep and to stay safe and warm. Even birds that do not generally use a nest box will retreat to a roosting box if the opportunity and conditions exist. Many of the larger birds such as flickers, Screech Owls, and kestrels prefer to sleep by themselves and will often use a nesting box throughout the year for shelter. But wrens, Downy Woodpeckers, titmice, chickadees, nuthatches, and many others will congregate in numbers in a roosting box on windy cold nights.

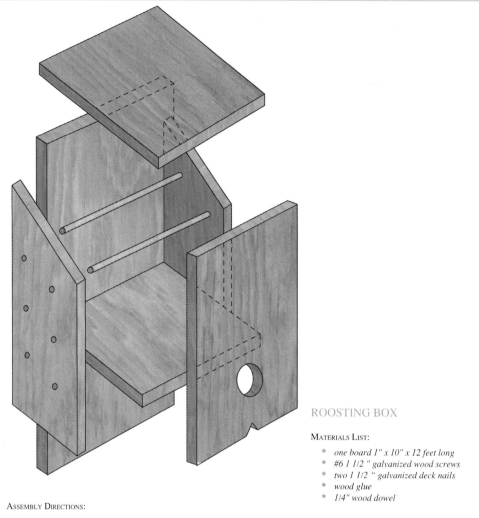

ROOSTING BOX

MATERIALS LIST:

* one board 1" x 10" x 12 feet long
* #6 1 1/2 " galvanized wood screws
* two 1 1/2 " galvanized deck nails
* wood glue
* 1/4" wood dowel

ASSEMBLY DIRECTIONS:

Do not include ventilation holes in a roosting box; this helps conserve heat during the winter cold.

1) *Measure and mark dimensions on board and cut out one piece at a time to allow for saw cut.*
2) *Mark on one side where perch holes will be located. Stagger holes to keep birds from roosting directly over each other. Lay both sides down together and drill holes for both sides at same time.*
3) *Fasten one side to bottom using wood glue on edge of board and two wood screws.*
4) *Attach back to bottom and side using three screws on side and two on bottom of back panel.*
5) *Cut dowel rods to length and insert with wood glue into assembled side of roosting box.*
6) *Assemble second side by lining up dowel rods into predrilled holes on side. Be sure to use wood glue in holes and then screw entire side into place with five wood screws.*
7) *Drill a 1 1/2" entrance hole in bottom of front panel and also cut notch for L-screw latch. Attach by using two galvanized decking nails to serve as pivot points and door hinge.*

1"X10"X12'

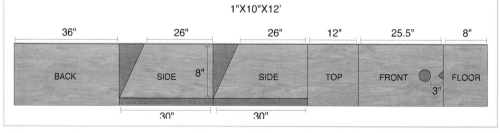

Roosting boxes should be constructed from the same quality materials as birdhouses and nesting boxes. To accommodate greater numbers of birds, roosting boxes are much larger than nesting boxes, usually about 10 inches square and as tall as 3 feet from bottom to top of roof. Because the heat from the birds' bodies will help to heat the inside of the structure, the entrance hole is made at the bottom of the box so that rising heat does not escape. The front, rather than the top, should be hinged for periodic inspections and cleaning. As shown in the illustration, stagger the perches all the way to the top so that individual birds are not roosting on top of each other.

Place the roosting box 8 to 10 feet above the ground, facing south to take advantage of the warm sun and opposite the winter northerly winds. A naturally sheltered place away from buildings or objects that cats can jump from is also recommended. Ideally, it should be mounted on a pole with a predator guard to keep cats, raccoons, and other predators from climbing into or reaching inside the box.

Natural Shelters

Many birds benefit from our manufactured and constructed bird homes. However, much of the existing vegetation and natural terrain around us are also valuable in the entire scheme of providing shelter for our feathered friends.

SNAGS

A dead tree, or "snag," is looked at by many homeowners as something that needs to be cut down for firewood. However, these dead, decaying trees provide food in the form of insects and insect larvae for more than 40 species of birds and other wildlife. Snags also provide birds with a place for nesting, perching, and roosting, and a place to establish territory.

Two different types of snags are used by birds. The first, called a soft snag, is a dead tree without limbs that is in an advanced stage of decomposition. The center of the tree is soft and easily breaks apart. The second type is called a hard snag and is also a dead tree, but it has some branches and is not in a rotted or decomposed state.

Both trees can be utilized by the homeowner for backyard birds. The ideal snag is usually 6 inches in diameter and approximately 10 to 15 feet high. It is usually the case that the bigger the snag, the greater benefit it will have to wildlife. Some backyard birdwatchers will cut soft snags and mount them on their property to attract woodpeckers. Hard snags can also be useful by providing additional perches and resting places for birds. Snags make excellent additions to feeding stations and great a place for mounting suet feeders; holes can even be drilled into the side of the snag in random locations and packed with suet.

Soft snags usually have numerous woodpecker holes in them and can sometimes be made into birdhouses for chickadees, nuthatches, and titmice. Depending on the state of decomposition and where the cavities are located, the snag can be sectioned into lengths and each section can be fitted with a sloped, bark-covered roof—the result is several natural birdhouses ready for mounting. An alternative would be to mount the entire snag in an appropriate location and let the birds pick their own home. Natural tree cavities are more attractive to certain species of birds than man-made birdhouses and add a rustic touch to a backyard bird sanctuary.

Snags can also be used to mount a constructed wooden birdhouse, rather than a steel or wooden post; this arrangement is often better received by some of the more finicky birds. Regardless of how they are used, with a little creativity snags can make a very natural-looking display in a nicely planted yard.

COMMON BIRDS THAT WILL USE SNAGS

Species	Nests in Cavity	Produces Cavity
Bluebirds	•	
Chickadees	•	•
Nuthatches	•	•
Titmice	•	
American Kestrel	•	
Barn Owl	•	
Screech Owl	•	
Barred Owl	•	
Saw-whet Owl	•	
Common Flicker	•	
Pileated Woodpecker	•	•
Red-bellied Woodpecker	•	•
Red-headed Woodpecker	•	•
Hairy Woodpecker	•	•
Downy Woodpecker	•	•
Great Crested Flycatcher	•	
Ash-throated Flycatcher	•	
Violet-green Swallow	•	
Tree Swallow	•	
Purple Martin	•	
Wrens	•	
European Starling	•	
House Sparrow	•	

BRUSH PILES AS SAFE HAVENS

For many homeowners, brush piles are considered an eyesore, but if you have an area on your property where tree branches seem to accumulate, this pile can be an added source of cover for many birds. Brush piles are also used by a number of other forms of wildlife such as garter snakes, lizards, woodchucks, skunks, cottontail rabbits, opossums, and even red foxes. In addition to providing cover from inclement weather, they also provide a means of escape from predators. Several ground-dwelling species of birds such as quail, pheasant, and grouse will quickly seek refuge from predators in a thick brush pile.

A simple pile of branches, however, does not always attract birds as a safe and sheltered place to retreat, nor does it qualify as a good brush pile. There are actually a right way and a wrong way to build a brush pile that will be used by many of the smaller species of songbirds as well as benefit other forms of wildlife.

Location must first be considered. Ideally, brush piles need to be situated in a sheltered area along the edges of grassy fields and woods; avoid placing them too close to your house because these piles also attract skunks and woodchucks. Keep in mind that the esthetic value of a pile of stumps, branches, and boughs is very limited—so limited, in fact, that neighbors might express their disapproval. Privacy fences or strategically placed shrubs and tall plants may sometimes remedy this portion of the problem.

Start the bottom of the brush pile with the larger and heavier materials. Heavy stumps and large rocks can be used to build a solid base and provide den sites for mammals. Continue with larger branches and limbs by criss-crossing them as you work your way up. Smaller lightweight branches should be added in the same manner, along with vines and finally evergreen branches on top. A larger limb or two can be placed at the very top to keep the whole pile from blowing apart. The finished product is usually about 5 feet in height and 10 to 15 feet in diameter. Of course, depending on the size of your yard, a smaller version can still be effective.

Many people will disassemble and burn the lighter portion of their brush pile each year before the nesting season begins. As the summer months proceed, new materials are added to begin the making of another pile for the fall and winter months

Brush piles may not be ideal for every backyard, but if the space warrants it, they are an ideal addition to any bird sanctuary.

> **RECYCLING TIP**
>
> If you use a live Christmas tree for your holiday celebrations, January is an ideal time to cut the evergreen boughs and add them to the top of your brush pile.

A carefully managed brush pile attracts birds all year, but it also can draw nuisance mammals if you are not careful.

Brown-headed Cowbirds are serious pests that often invade nesting boxes as well as natural nests.

Chapter Six

Problem Solving

Competition for Nest Space

You've created the perfect backyard sanctuary by providing birds with their four basic needs. Food, water, shelter, and space have all attributed to your success with an active and well-received birdhouse program. Yet, by creating this successful backyard bird habitat, you've also created habitat for other creatures as well.

Other Birds

One of the most important things you can do as a wild bird landlord is to try to keep out nesting site competitors such as House Sparrows and European Starlings. Not only can they occupy valuable nesting sites intended for other birds, but they can also puncture eggs, kill young birds, and destroy entire nests.

However, competitor bird species are not always House Sparrows and starlings. House Wrens, chickadees, titmice, Tree Swallows, and even bluebirds can be considered competitors if you are trying to attract a different species of bird.

When trying to cut back on nesting box intrusions, there are several areas you can investigate. First look at the specifications of the house you built. Be sure the entrance hole size and the other dimensions are exactly correct. If there are inaccuracies to be corrected, this will in many cases automatically eliminate some of the competitors, or it will determine if the house should be designated for another species.

Because House Sparrows are introduced birds, they carry no legal protection at the state or federal level. Destroying nests, moving nests, and even trapping all can be used to control House Sparrow problems.

Check the location and confirm that it is in the proper habitat. Consider food sources, clearings, trees and shrubs, and any other variables required of the desired species. Is it mounted at the correct height and facing the right direction?

Timing may also be an issue. Different migratory birds arrive at different times during the spring. Some species of local birds also nest at different times during a nesting season. If birdhouses are out ahead of the intended birds' arrival, closing off the holes until that time will prohibit unwelcome visitors. As the intended birds arrive, the holes can then be opened for their use.

Another method in controlling starlings and sparrows is to continually remove their nesting material, thus discouraging their nesting and their presence. Male House Sparrows are very territorial, however, and can be difficult to encourage to nest somewhere else. Sometimes by uprooting a pair of nesting sparrows, you send them to another already occupied nest box, creating a new set of problems. A final option for especially destructive birds may be to live-trap them (consult with your local wildlife authorities) and attempt to relocate them.

Note that House Wrens are federally protected birds (unlike European Stalings and House Sparrows) and neither the nests and eggs nor the adults may be disturbed. The only thing you can do is put up several houses specifically designed for wrens and hope they take up residency in one of them.

MICE

Mice typically take up residency in the late fall or winter months, building their winter nests in empty birdhouses for protection from the upcoming cold weather. As harmless as that may seem, in the springtime these pests become competitors for the birds' nesting sites. To take care of the problem, homeowners can either let them be and evict them before the onset of the breeding season, close off the entrance hole for the winter, or totally remove the house until spring.

WASPS AND BEES

Wasps and bees will also nest in empty boxes. Although there have been cases of wasps stinging and killing birds when both wasps and birds attempt to nest at the same time, this is not the norm. The best way to keep them from occupying the nest is to coat the inside top of the birdhouse with regular bar soap. The soap will keep the wasps from attaching their nests to the top of the box, but it will not harm the birds.

Bees and wasps of many types find the dark recesses of a nesting box attractive. Never use insecticides in your attempts to evict them.

Evicting an existing wasp or bee nest requires extra precautions. Some people recommend leaving the nest until fall, when it can safely be disposed of. Others will aggressively evict the wasps and hope not to be stung.

Insecticides should not be used because of the risk they pose to adults or young birds.

ASSEMBLY
1) Slide pipe over post.
2) Mount bird house.

Predators and Pests

Nesting birds are extremely vulnerable to predators, which is one reason that so much thought should go into the actual placement of a nesting box. Certain steps can be taken to prevent unwanted predators from destroying nests, eggs, fledglings, and adult birds. The most common predators of birdhouses include raccoons, cats, opossums, and snakes. Some common competitors for nesting space—insects, wrens, House Sparrows, and squirrels—are also predators. At times grackles, jays, crows, and even chipmunks will prey on nesting birds for eggs.

Roaming house cats may be the most serious danger you will face at your nesting boxes. Cats soon learn the habits of local birds and will wait for a chance to grab a quick snack; fledglings are especially likely to be killed.

CATS

The house cat is considered by many backyard birdwatchers to be a bird's worse enemy. Cats, which are extremely agile climbers and jumpers, are excellent stalkers that when allowed to roam outdoors will freely prey upon both baby and adult birds.

Several things can be checked if you are faced with cats preying upon the birdhouses and birds in your yard. First, be sure your birdhouses are situated away from any limbs and buildings that could act as a springboard for cats to pounce from. Clear away unnecessary vegetation, fences, or blind spots that cats could hide behind when stalking birds near the nesting area. If cats are visible to the birds, their chances of success are drastically reduced. Declawed cats and cats wearing bells still make quite capable hunters, so don't count on these approaches as solutions.

Pole-mounted birdhouses should have a PVC pipe or sheet metal band around the post to prevent cats from climbing. Metal cone guards installed on poles also serve the same purpose as well as helping prevent jumping.

Perhaps the most surefire method in controlling cat predation is to keep your cat inside. Obviously, this may work for your cat but not for any other neighborhood cats on the prowl.

RACCOONS

The raccoon, appropriately referred to by many as the "masked bandit," is one of the most common problematic wild animals faced by birding landlords. Although raccoons are generally woodland cavity-nesting animals, occupying similar habitats to that of many of our songbirds, they are quite comfortable in rural and even urban neighborhoods. Like cats and squirrels, raccoons are capable and agile climbers. These remarkably strong animals can destroy birdhouses and entire nests, as well as devour eggs, young, and adult birds.

Adult raccoons can weigh as much as 30 pounds. Because of this creature's strength, weight, and dexterity, birdhouses need to be properly constructed and securely fastened when mounted on poles and trees. A predator guard should be built around the entrance hole using a block of wood $^3/_4$-inch thick (the diameter of the predator guard hole should match the diameter of the birdhouse entrance hole). This extra precaution makes it more difficult for the raccoon to reach into the entrance and disturb the nest. An additional guard can be constructed from $^1/_4$-inch hardware cloth. It should be cut approximately 4 by 10 inches and shaped into a rectangular form and stapled around the

Raccoons may enter backyards, even in cities, and will simply tear a box apart to get at the sleeping birds. They also are important carriers of rabies in some parts of the country. There may be little you can do to deter a determined raccoon.

entrance hole, creating a tunnel effect (see illustration). The outside is left with the jagged points facing out to further deter the raccoon's paws.

As with cats, installing sheet metal guards, sheet metal cones, and PVC pipes around the mounting post will help to deter climbing raccoons. Coating the mounting post with petroleum jelly, oil, grease, Teflon spray, or any other slippery substance is typically of little use—other than to create a very slippery predator.

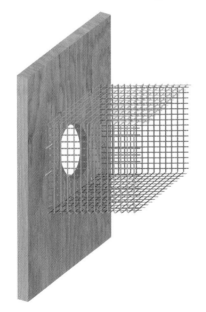

ASSEMBLY
1) *Using 1/4" hardware cloth, cut a strip 4" x 10 to16" in length, depending on the entrance hole size.*
2) *Bend the strip into a rectangular shape that will fit around the outside entrance hole, leaving the jagged edges facing out.*
3) *The entire piece is stapled to the front of the box forming a tunnel effect for the bird to enter, also leaving a difficult entrance for predator paws.*

Opossums

The North American opossum is not as great of a threat to nesting birds as the cat or raccoon. Although opossums will feed on eggs and fledglings when they can get to them, they will generally first scavenge for anything else they can find. Opossums can climb, but they are not nearly as agile as the raccoon and they are easily discouraged with the same predator guards and precautions as described for the raccoon.

57

There are many species of squirrels and chipmunks in the U.S. and Canada, and most have a tendency to become nuisances when you feed birds or offer nesting boxes. Squirrels are attractive animals with many friends, however, and often it is best to simply accept them and just give them enough food to keep them occupied.

SQUIRRELS AND CHIPMUNKS

Squirrels and chipmunks serve as another menace to birdhouse landlords. These crafty creatures will invade a birdhouse and eat the eggs and even very small baby birds.

When an entrance hole has been chewed and enlarged it is usually the work of a squirrel. Entrance holes may be protected by cutting hardware cloth or sheet metal to fit around the nest box hole, which should prevent the squirrel from chewing through.

Like cats, squirrels are excellent climbers and jumpers. Squirrel baffles and predator guards will help to prevent access

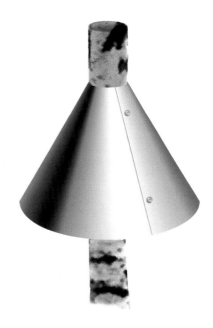

on post-mounted birdhouses, assuming the house is located high enough that they cannot jump to it. Again, properly situating the house in an area free of branches and away from trees, ledges, or buildings will keep jumping to a minimum.

Chipmunks are not the avid climbers that squirrels are. They will climb to and frequent birdfeeders when possible, often hoarding as much seed as they can manage; they may also steal eggs from nest boxes. Generally, a squirrel baffle or predator guard on the post is enough to deter them.

ASSEMBLY
1) *The best results for a cone guard are achieved by starting with a square piece of sheet metal and then cut it into a circular shape.*
2) *Cut out a 3" tapered notch and hole in the center, large enough to accommodate post.*
3) *Drill four holes in sheet metal.*
4) *Cone is wrapped around post and tightly bolted together with two bolts to hold cone in place.*

Racers and other snakes sometimes enter nesting boxes to feed on eggs, nestlings, and even adults. Bluebird trails in open country are especially subject to their depredations. It may take considerable experimentation with the width of a predator guard before you can keep snakes out of a box.

SNAKES

Several species of snakes readily prey upon nesting birds. Because snakes do no damage to a box itself, their presence often goes undetected, other than disappearing eggs or baby birds. Snakes such as Corn Snakes, Yellow Rat Snakes, Black Rat Snakes, racers, Fox Snakes, Kingsnakes, water snakes, and sometimes garter snakes can all be threats to nesting birds. They are excellent climbers and are not deterred by poles.

The best predator guards for snakes are the stovepipe and cone-shaped guards used against many of the other ground-dwelling and climbing animals. However, unlike other animals, snakes are capable of extending their bodies out horizontally to go around and over ledges. If you live in a region where snakes are a problem, it is highly recommended that you increase the size of a cone-shaped guard to 36 to 40 inches in diameter. Occasionally a snake may be found in a nest box after eating a meal. If this is the case, gently remove it with a stick and set it free. Snakes are an important part of an ecosystem and should not be harmed.

ASSEMBLY
1) Measure tree diameter with a piece of string and add 2".
2) Cut a piece of sheet metal 36" x above dimension.
3) Mark and drill bolt holes.
4) Wrap around tree and tighten snugly.

Gopher Snakes and most other bird-eaters have amazingly flexible, muscular bodies that allow them to climb almost any surface.

Other Problems

NUISANCE WILDLIFE

Well-balanced ecosystems and habitats may also invite animals other than birds that we may not be interested in. Nuisance wildlife are usually categorized as the animals that are raiding feeders, vegetable or flower gardens, or birdhouses or are destructive in some manner. If they cannot be controlled by predator guards, baffles, or natural strategies such as creative placement and construction techniques, they can sometimes be captured and relocated to another area. Live-capture traps are most commonly used for raccoons, skunk, opossums, woodchucks, squirrels, chipmunks, sparrows, starlings, and pigeons. This method should be a last alternative for problematic animals and should first be discussed with your local and state authorities.

Live-trapping animals from your property can be an effective method for removing destructive animals. However, it is important to remember that there is a natural balance in any healthy ecosystem, and by removing animals you also create a natural vacuum for new ones to move in. It is far better to control nuisance wildlife by natural methods rather than trying to relocate them.

BIRDS ABANDON OR WON'T USE HOUSING

Usually, if a bird won't use a birdhouse, the process of elimination can be used to determine the cause. Is the species of bird prevalent in your area? Look at the actual dimensions and materials of the house. Are they correct and accurate for the species of bird you are trying to attract? What about the color of the birdhouse? Is it white for martins and a natural color for other cavity-nesting birds?

DEADLY DUST

Diatomaceous earth is a natural product successfully used in controlling parasites in a nest box. Simply sprinkle a teaspoon of powder inside around the edges of the box. It can be used at any stage of nesting and will kill any existing insects. This substance is derived from tiny marine animals called diatoms, which are ground into a fine powder; this dust contains extremely sharp fine particles that cut into the exoskeletons of the insects, causing them to die.

A natural method of parasite control for Purple Martin colonies is to frequently change the nesting material. This method has proven safe and successful for minimizing infestations and will not cause abandonment of the nest or any ill harm to the nestlings. Simply remove the chicks and gently place them into a soft box or holding container and remove the old nest material and replace it with new, clean, dry nesting material. Replacement material can be lawn clippings, pine needles, straw, or pine chips. Nestlings should be at least ten days old when this is done; the process can be repeated when they are about 18 to 20 days old. This method has worked well for martins, but should not be used with other cavity-nesting birds. The nesting material for all other cavity-nesting birds should be discarded only after each clutch is raised.

Lurking predators will cause a house not to be used or to be abandoned if the birds feel threatened. Be sure there are no bushes, fences, or hidden corners that a cat or other predator could be hiding behind while waiting for a meal.

If you've gone through the correct steps in construction, try relocating it or installing another one. Always give the birds some time, at least two weeks, before trying a new location.

PARASITES

Many parasites nuisance insects lay their eggs in nesting boxes, and being aware of them is half the battle. Ants, gypsy moths, blowflies, wasps, bees, spiders, lice, and mites may all potentially invade a nesting box. Sometimes they can be seen during visual inspections, but at other times their presence will go unknown.

The best treatment against parasites is preventative maintenance. Pyrethrin-based insecticides and 1% rotenone when applied at the end of every breeding season will kill almost all insects, and arachnids, plus their eggs and larvae, resulting in a parasite-free house for the next season. In addition, coating the top inside of the box with regular bar soap will help to prevent infestations of wasps and bees.

Blowflies lay their eggs in nest boxes of almost all cavity-nesting birds. These eggs hatch into larvae and the larvae attach themselves to the nestlings, feeding on their blood. The blowfly larvae are generally translucent in color, $1/4$ to $1/2$ inch in length, but they will take on a reddish color after feeding. If found, they should be removed and destroyed.

Most birds have at least some lice, and these can become a problem by the end of each nesting. Each time you clean the box, an application of a natural insecticide will kill any insect parasites present and may reduce the number that take up residence later in the season.

RESOURCES

Books

HOW BIRDS WORK: A GUIDE TO BIRD BIOLOGY
Ron Freethy
Blandford Press, 1982.

ATTRACTING BACKYARD BIRDS: INVITING PROJECTS TO ENTICE YOUR FEATHERED FRIENDS
Sandy Cortright and WillPokriots
Sterling, 1995.

BIRDS IN THE GARDEN
Mike Mockler
Sterling, 1982.

LANDSCAPING FOR WILDLIFE
Carrol L. Henderson
Minnesota Department of Natural Resources, 1987.

SONGBIRDS IN YOUR GARDEN
John K. Terres
Algonquin Books, of Chapel Hill, 1994.

THAYER BIRDING SOFTWARE'S BIRDS OF NORTH AMERICA
[interactive multimedia]
Thayer Birding Software, 1998.

BLUEBIRDS: SYMBOL OF HOPE
Steve Grooms and Dick Peterson
NorthWord Press, 1991.

THE BACKYARD BIRDWATCHER
George H.Harrison
Simon and Schuster, 1979.

STOKES PURPLE MARTIN BOOK: THE COMPLETE GUIDE TO ATTRACTING AND HOUSING PURPLE MARTINS
Justin L. Brown and Donald and Lillian Strokes
Little, Brown and Co., 1997.

STOKES FIELD GUIDE TO BIRDS
(WESTERN AND EASTERN REGIONS)
Donald and Lillian Strokes
Little, Brown and Co., 1996.

AMERICA'S FAVORITE BACKYARD BIRDS
Kit and George Harrison
Simon and Schuster, 1983.

Internet Information

BIRD LINKS TO THE WORLD
www.ntic.qc.ca/~nellus

BIRD SOURCE/CORNELL LABORATORY OF ORNITHOLOGY
www.birdsource.cornell.edu/index.html

NORTHERN PRAIRIE WILDLIFE RESEARCH CENTER
www.npwrc.usgs.gov/index.htm

U.S. FISH AND WILDLIFE SERVICE
www.fws.gov/

INDEX

Page numbers in **bold** indicate photos

How Can I Help?
Friends Helping Friends™

HELPING A FRIEND WHO IS BEING BULLIED

Corona Brezina

ROSEN PUBLISHING

New York

Published in 2017 by The Rosen Publishing Group, Inc.
29 East 21st Street, New York, NY 10010

Library of Congress Cataloging-in-Publication Data

Names: Brezina, Corona, author.
Title: Helping a friend who is being bullied / Corona Brezina.
Description: First edition. | New York : Rosen Publishing, 2017. | Series: How can I help? Friends helping friends | Includes bibliographical references and index.
Identifiers: LCCN 2016017417 | ISBN 9781499464542 (library bound) | ISBN 9781499464528 (pbk.) | ISBN 9781499464535 (6-pack)
Subjects: LCSH: Bullying—Prevention—Juvenile literature. | Bullying—Juvenile literature. | Bullying in schools—Juvenile literature.
Classification: LCC BF637.B85 B74 2017 | DDC 302.34/3—dc23
LC record available at https://lccn.loc.gov/2016017417

Manufactured in China

CONTENTS

INTRODUCTION

It's a scenario that's played out every day in the United States, in every state, and probably in your own school. One kid—the bully—is bigger or more popular or more aggressive than most of the other students. He or she targets a victim, perhaps physically, perhaps by taunting or spreading rumors behind the victim's back. Whatever the approach, the victim is unable to defend him- or herself, and the attacks continue. But there's a third role in the scenario: that played by the bystander, or witness. The bystander's actions can be crucial in determining the outcome of the situation. Does the bystander join the bully, remain neutral, or defend the victim?

Bullying is a serious and widespread problem. A 2014 report by the US Department of Education found that 22 percent of students ages twelve to eighteen had experienced bullying. More girls than boys reported that they'd been bullied, but boys were more often the victims of physical bullying. About 7 percent of students reported that they had been the victims of cyberbullying.

If you have a friend who is being bullied, you're undoubtedly anxious, indignant, and saddened on his or her behalf. If this person is a close friend, you may be eager to help him or her but unsure of what you can do. Even

Being bullied can make young people feel like they're utterly alone. Having a supportive friend can help a victim cope through the ordeal.

when you see others bullied who are only casual acquaintances, you may feel guilty about failing to take action to help the victim.

One of the best ways you can help your friend is simply by staying true and continuing to extend your friendship. One common trait of many bullying victims is that they're socially isolated. Maybe they're shy. Maybe they have trouble relating to their peers. Having supportive friends, though, can buffer kids from being bullied.

You can also help your friend identify resources and allies that can help him or her recover from the traumatic experience. Kids are sometimes reluctant to "tattle" on their peers. For a serious matter such as bullying, however, informing an adult is not "tattling," it's reporting. Bullying can cause both short-term and long-term emotional damage that can have aftereffects that last a lifetime.

Urge your friend to tell his or her parents about the bullying. They can support their child and offer guidance for dealing with the situation. Teachers and school authorities can work to halt the bullying. In extreme cases, the police may get involved, as well. Mental health professionals such as therapists, psychologists, psychiatrists, and counselors can help your friend recover from the bullying.

Timely intervention can help your friend regain his or her confidence and happiness and prevent any lasting impact from the bullying. Promoting a bully-free learning environment, as well, will benefit the entire school.

CHAPTER ONE

RECOGNIZING BULLYING

Bullying is aggressive behavior often directed toward targets who are unable to defend themselves or retaliate. Spats and mild teasing are typical among peers, but bullies go out of their way to

Bullying can erode a victim's self-esteem and lead to a sense of rejection at a stage in life when young people yearn to be accepted by their peers.

target specific victims. Some bullying is overt—if you have a friend who has been shoved or taunted, you would certainly acknowledge the behavior as bullying. But what about more subtle attacks, such as malicious gossip or relentless teasing that the perpetrator insists is all in fun? The first step in helping a friend who is being bullied is recognizing the bullying.

Bullying involves a pattern of intentionally hurtful behavior that occurs repeatedly. There's usually an imbalance of power in a bullying situation. The bully may be bigger, older, more aggressive, or more popular. The bullying is deliberate, not the result of thoughtlessness or roughhousing. The bully chooses a specific target, deliberately inflicts hurt, and enjoys seeing the victim suffer. In addition, it's not a one-time occurrence. The bully and target both expect that the bullying will happen again. This prospect can instill a sense of dread in the victim that can't be escaped.

TYPES OF BULLYING

The most recognizable form of bullying is physical. A larger kid may shove, trip, hit, or pinch the victim. He or she might pull the victim's hair or throw spitballs. Physical bullying also includes threatening gestures or intimidation, such as violating personal space. Stealing or damaging property qualifies as physical bullying, too. The bully might demand money or trash a homework assignment. Physical bullying is the type that's most likely to grab adult attention and lead to disciplinary action, because it causes visible signs—injuries and damage to clothing or belongings—as well as mental distress.

Physical bullying is not the same as a fight between two kids. There's an imbalance of power, such as when two boys target someone who's smaller.

A bully doesn't have to use force or even the threat of violence to inflict pain on a victim, though. The most common kind of bullying is verbal abuse, in which the bully uses words as weapons. Verbal bullying includes name-calling, insults, and intimidation. A bully might target someone's appearance, race, sexual orientation, or personal idiosyncrasies. Verbal bullying can be more difficult for teachers and other adults to recognize, and it's easier for the bully to deny. Nonetheless, verbal bullying can be devastating for a kid's confidence and self-esteem.

Another type of bullying is social or relational bullying, in which the victim is isolated and shunned. At an age when young people tend to want to fit in with the crowd, the victim is made to feel like he or she is all alone. The other kids might exclude the victim from activities, spread rumors behind his or her back, or inflict public humiliation. The bully might pressure the victim's friends into abandoning him or her. If you have a friend who is experiencing relational bullying, you can combat bullying simply by continuing to extend your friendship and refusing to ostracize your friend. As with verbal bullying, it can be hard for the victim to prove that he or she is being singled out for social or relational bullying.

These different types of bullying tend to overlap and escalate. Verbal bullying can lead to physical bullying, for example, or an incident can involve elements of all three kinds of bullying.

IS A FRIEND BEING BULLIED?

Even if you know enough to recognize the different types of bullying when you see them occur, you still might not realize that your friend is being bullied if you don't witness it directly. Maybe the bullying occurs when you're not around your friend, and he or she is unwilling to tell you about it. There are many reasons that your friend could be reluctant to speak up. It could be that your friend is ashamed of being bullied and is afraid that you might think less of him or her for being unable to put a stop to it. Perhaps your friend is afraid to tell an adult about the bullying and believes that you might urge him or her to report it.

Kids respond to bullying in various ways depending on their personality. Some young people fight back, while

CYBERBULLYING

Until the past couple of decades, young people could escape bullies once they were out of sight. This practice has changed with the internet age and the new phenomenon of cyberbullying, in which the bullies use technology to target their victims. Cyberbullying often occurs through social media such as Facebook and Twitter; other means include texts, email, instant messaging, chat rooms, message boards, and various cell phone apps. Cyberbullies often harass their victims by sending taunting messages and spreading rumors—much like verbal bullying—but technology provides new weapons for bullies. They can post hurtful photos and videos that are difficult to remove once published and shared. The internet offers anonymity as well. Cyberbullies can hide their identity, impersonate the victim online to humiliate him or her, or pose as someone else in order to trick their target. Cyberbullying can be devastating for the victim, and the consequences of cyberbullying are likely to become ever more prevalent as electronic media become more and more important in kids' daily lives.

others accept the bullying and become withdrawn. There are many other warning signs that a kid is a victim of bullying, as well. You might notice bruises or ripped clothes or observe his or her possessions go missing. Your friend might suddenly change routine, probably to avoid places and

Being bullied can make the victim feel like he's all alone, which may lead to noticeable changes in mood and actions.

situations where he or she might fear being targeted by a bully. Kids who are being cyberbullied may appear anxious when they check their social media accounts or texts. If you observe any of these changes in your friend's behavior, it could be a reaction to being bullied.

The psychological stress inflicted by bullying can take a toll on the victim's health, and your friend might start suffering from unexplained illnesses such as stomachaches or other types of pain. When bullying is really bad, kids sometimes start skipping school or think about running away.

MYTHS AND FACTS

MYTH: Getting bullied toughens kids up, or bullying builds character.

FACT: Bullying can cause serious damage to a young person's self-esteem. It can make it harder for him or her to cope with the daily problems of life. Bullying weakens and harms the targets.

MYTH: Bystanders are neutral.

FACT: If you witness bullying and do nothing about it, you are participating in it. Bullies enjoy an audience.

MYTH: Telling an adult about bullying will only make the situation worse.

FACT: Parents, teachers, and other adults can intervene and support the victim. Adults have a responsibility to help a victim who feels isolated, helpless, hopeless, and miserable because of a bully's behavior.

CHAPTER TWO

UNDERSTANDING THE CONSEQUENCES OF BULLYING

E ven if you recognize bullying, you might tell yourself that it's not a big deal. Bullying is a rotten experience, but plenty of kids go through it with no harm done, right? On the contrary, bullying can cause damage persisting over a lifetime. Even some celebrities—from comedian Chris Rock to actress Jennifer Lawrence—look back at the experience of being bullied as an obstacle that they had to overcome on their path to success. In some extreme cases, however, bullying can lead to tragedy. If you have a friend being bullied, your support could mean a lot to him or her.

DAMAGE DONE BY BULLYING

In the short-term, bullying can make the victim physically sick. Bullying causes stress, and the body responds to stress with the "fight or flight" response. Human beings developed this reaction in order to provide extra strength and awareness in times of acute danger. The heart rate accelerates and pupils dilate, for example, to provide peak physical performance. Once the threat abates, the body returns to normal. But modern-day stressors such as bullying can create a state of chronic stress. A young person who is being bullied can't relax and destress. That's why bullying victims report physical symptoms such as loss of appetite, fatigue, and headaches.

Bullying victims also experience psychological and emotional consequences. Kids who are bullied feel anger, frustration, hopelessness, and bewilderment. Shy kids may become even more withdrawn; outgoing kids may erupt in rage easily. Bullying victims are at a higher risk for mental health issues such as anxiety, panic attacks, and depression. The bullying also eats away at their confidence and

Bullies tend to pick on peers who react fearfully on being confronted. A confident attitude can help a target avoid becoming a frequent victim of bullying.

self-esteem. Bullying victims sometimes develop "learned helplessness," in which they believe that they have no means of changing their situation, even if it isn't true.

THE CONSEQUENCES FOR THE BULLY

Believe it or not, bullies suffer repercussions from their own behavior as well. Most discussion of bullying focuses on the harm done to the victim, and it's hard to feel sympathy for someone who takes pleasure in inflicting pain on vulnerable peers. But bullies are also subject to long-term negative consequences associated with bullying others.

There's no single reason that explains why kids turn into bullies. Often, though, bullies come from family environments in which bullying occurred, and they follow the example shown during their upbringing. Bullies sometimes have trouble building healthy relationships with their peers, and they tend to overstep the boundaries of rules and social norms.

At school, bullies might get away with this behavior. Later in life, they face the consequences. Former bullies are at a higher risk of abusing drugs and alcohol, and they tend to engage in sexual activity at an earlier age. They're more likely to get into fights, drop out of school, commit vandalism or other crimes, and abuse their future partners and children. All of these factors can limit future career and life opportunities as adults.

Bullying also has social consequences for the victim. Kids who are being bullied feel alienated and isolated from their peers. As the persecution continues, they find it hard to trust other kids or the adults who failed to prevent the bullying. A bullying victim might push away friends, or he or she may have problems making friends. Prolonged bullying can impact a kid's ability to form interpersonal relationships. If you have a friend who is retreating into silence and dejection, especially if you've witnessed him or her being bullied, try to reach out and find out what's wrong.

Someone who's being bullied can have trouble concentrating on schoolwork. Pressure about school performance by teachers and parents may add to the person's feelings of stress and anxiety.

These physical, emotional, and social consequences can affect a student's performance at school. For a bullying victim, schoolwork may start to seem like a low priority compared to planning strategies to ensure personal safety. He or she may feel too sick and anxious to concentrate on homework and too intimidated to participate in class activities. The victim's grades may start to slip. He or she might start skipping school. Studies have shown that kids who are bullied are more likely to drop out of school.

Some bullying victims are damaged for life by the experience. Adults who were bullied as children remain at a higher risk for anxiety and depression. They may tend to be loners or have trouble forming close relationships. They may be overly sensitive to criticism and aggressiveness. Low grades during high school can lead to academic difficulties in college and even affect career prospects.

EXTREME CASES

Bullying can sometimes drive victims to take drastic actions. Young people who have been bullied are more likely to have suicidal thoughts and feelings, and some bullying victims

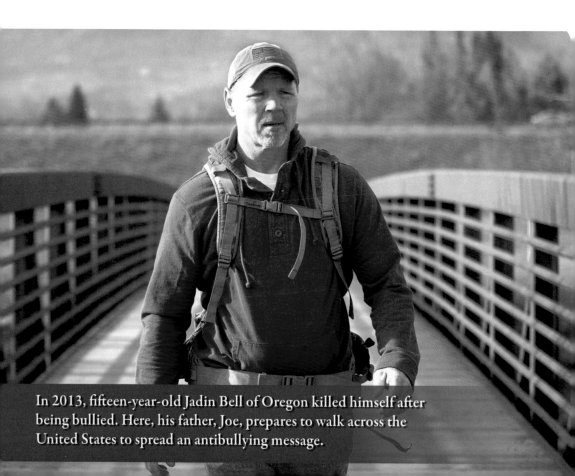

In 2013, fifteen-year-old Jadin Bell of Oregon killed himself after being bullied. Here, his father, Joe, prepares to walk across the United States to spread an antibullying message.

even take their own lives. These cases are very rare, although such incidents of "bullycide" tend to be widely reported and discussed in the media. Nonetheless, bullying generally isn't the sole contributing factor in such deaths. The victims tend to struggle with other issues, such as family trouble or mental illness. But bullying can make these difficult situations even worse.

There is also a link between bullying and school shootings. A study by the US Secret Service found that one of the few common factors among school shooters was a background of being bullied. Once again, it's very rare for bullying victims to retaliate with this degree of violence.

These incidents are rare occurrences, but they vividly demonstrate the damage that can be done by bullying. If you have a friend who mentions suicidal thoughts or talks about taking drastic revenge on bullies, tell a teacher, parent, or other school official. It's important that your friend get help.

CHAPTER THREE

WHY IS YOUR FRIEND BEING BULLIED?

"Why me?" a bullying victim might ask. Victims often experience feelings of anger, frustration, and hopelessness without really understanding why they were being singled out for bullying in the first place. Sometimes, kids put on a brave face to peers and pretend that nothing is wrong even when they're hurting inside.

You may know your friend to be a talented and engaging individual, but to the bully, he or she is just a target. Maybe the bully fixates on specific personal traits, or maybe your friend was just in the wrong place at the wrong time. Regardless, there's no valid justification for bullying—kids should never suffer simply for being different.

IT'S ALL ABOUT POWER

Bullying involves an imbalance of power between the bully and victim. The bully sees the victim as vulnerable—he or she may be small, quiet, or sensitive. When most people envision a bullying scenario, they picture a larger boy physically tormenting a smaller one. But size and strength isn't the only advantage a bully holds over the victim. A bully might possess information hurtful to the victim and be willing to share it by spreading rumors. A cyberbully can make the victim feel like there's no place or time where he or she can ever feel safe.

Bullies often pick on the kids who are different from the rest of the crowd. They may single out targets based on their race, ethnicity, or sexual orientation—lesbian, gay, bisexual, or transgender (LGBT) youth are at a high risk of being bullied. Kids might be targeted for their physical traits; academically gifted students might be bullied for being brainy. Low-income kids are at a higher risk of being

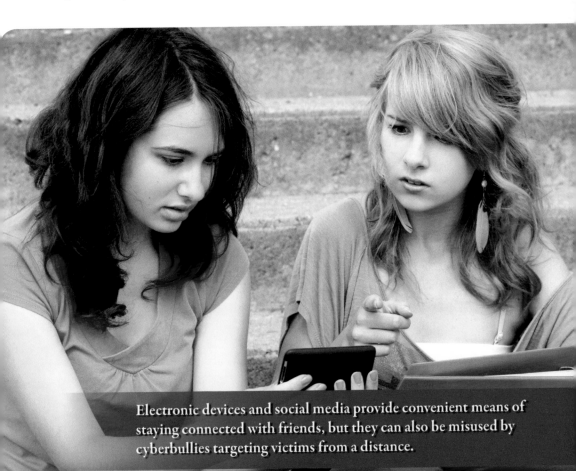

Electronic devices and social media provide convenient means of staying connected with friends, but they can also be misused by cyberbullies targeting victims from a distance.

bullied. They aren't targeted specifically for being poor, but they might not wear brand-name clothes or be able to afford school trips or activities such as sports. Children

IT REALLY DOES GET BETTER FOR LGBT YOUTH

LGBT youth are at a higher risk of bullying than average adolescents, and it can take a toll on their well-being. LGBT teens are also more likely to suffer from depression, substance abuse, and suicidal thoughts. In a supportive environment, however, LGBT students thrive.

In 2010, author and gay activist Dan Savage posted an online video telling young people that "it got better" in time. He was motivated to spread the message after high-profile suicides of LGBT youth who had been bullied. As he wrote in a column, "I wish I could have talked to this kid for five minutes. I wish I could have told Billy that *it gets better.*" Subsequently, many more activists, celebrities, and ordinary people posted their own It Gets Better videos—even Barack Obama assured kids that "it gets better."

Since then, It Gets Better has grown into an organization dedicated to fighting intolerance. The project's mission is "to communicate to lesbian, gay, bisexual, and transgender youth around the world that it gets better, and to create and inspire the changes needed to make it better for them."

with physical or mental abilities often find themselves the targets of bullies. They may stand out because of their appearance or behavior—people with autism may have trouble reading social cues, for example.

Regardless of the reason for choosing a target, the bully takes advantage of the victim's fear. If the victim responds fearfully during the first encounter, the bully is more likely to pick on the victim repeatedly. If the victim instead reacts assertively or walks away without showing fear, he or she may be able to avoid escalation of the bullying.

As mentioned, victims often become passive and withdrawn as a result of bullying. Some victims, however, react by lashing out. These confrontational victims tend to

Experts advise against trying to fight back against a bully, but an assertive reaction can sometimes demonstrate to a bully that his or her target isn't intimidated by the behavior.

be disruptive and have trouble connecting with peers, who may believe that the victim was asking for trouble through his or her behavior.

A common factor for bullying victims is social isolation. Whatever the reason, they lack the support of friends. Bullying can create a cycle of alienation for the victim, since it becomes harder for him or her to make new friends. Other kids may start to see the victim as a target, as well.

For many bullying victims, life gets easier once they're out of high school and can choose their own college and social circle. There, friends and peers will recognize them as special, talented individuals, not "different" people to single out for bullying. If you have a friend who is being bullied because of his or her identity or personal traits, remind your friend not to allow the bully's actions to affect his or her sense of self-worth.

BULLYING ROLES

Bullying scenarios are more complicated than just "bully" versus "victim." The federal government's website on bullying, stopbullying.gov, suggests referring to "the child who bullied" and "the child who was bullied" rather than describing them as "bully" and "victim." These labels send the message that their roles are fixed. The "bully" might be less likely to try to change his or her behavior. The "victim" might be less likely to reach out for support or try strategies for coping. In addition, both individuals involved are more complex than merely being "bully" and "victim."

Bullying victims may be tempted to retaliate by lashing out at their tormentors or at other students, which can have the effect of further alienating peers.

Labels oversimplify the real dynamics among peers. Roles can change and kids can take on different roles in different contexts. An unfortunate aspect of bullying is that victims sometimes respond by becoming bullies themselves. These "bully-victims" seek revenge on their tormentors by taking on some of the same behaviors that hurt them in the first place. Later in life, they tend to have more severe psychological difficulties than either bullies or victims on their own. If you have a friend who reacts to bullying by bullying others, urge him or her to resist the temptation to lash out. Tell your friend that there are resources that can help him or her recover from the experience.

10 GREAT QUESTIONS TO ASK A GUIDANCE COUNSELOR

1 HOW DO BULLIES CHOOSE THEIR TARGETS?

2 WHAT IS THE DIFFERENCE BETWEEN A PHYSICAL CONFLICT AND PHYSICAL BULLYING?

3 IS THERE A DIFFERENCE BETWEEN VERBAL BULLYING AND TEASING?

4 WHAT ARE THE SIGNS OF RELATIONAL BULLYING?

5 HOW CAN I PROTECT MYSELF AGAINST CYBERBULLYING?

6 WHAT CAN A BYSTANDER DO TO HELP IN A BULLYING SITUATION?

7 WHAT RESOURCES DOES MY SCHOOL PROVIDE FOR BULLYING VICTIMS?

8 WHERE CAN I GET A COPY OF MY SCHOOL'S POLICY ON BULLYING?

9 HOW CAN BULLYING VICTIMS HEAL AND RETURN TO A NORMAL LIFE?

10 WHAT IS THE DIFFERENCE BETWEEN BULLYING AND HARASSMENT?

CHAPTER FOUR

ARE YOU THE BYSTANDER?

I n many bullying situations, other kids look on while the bully goes after his or her victim. The bystander plays the third role in a bullying situation. If there are other young people present, the bully often puts on a show for the audience. He or she expects that the bystanders will either encourage the behavior or at least avoid taking sides. In turn, if nobody speaks up to condemn the behavior, the bystanders will be more likely to think that bullying is OK and imitate it.

If you see a friend being bullied, you may be tempted to think that there's nothing you can do to help. But because failing to speak up reinforces the message that bullying is acceptable, the bystander's role is very important. After all, a bystander has to make the decision not to intervene.

NOT JUST STANDING BY

Most bystanders aren't altogether neutral. Bystanders can play a number of roles, ranging from sidekicks of the bully to defenders of the victim. Many observers

For a victim of bullying, having peers looking on who are indifferent or actively participating in the bullying can make an incident even more painful.

feel uncomfortable watching a bully target a victim, but they end up participating against their will. It's sometimes said that there are no innocent bystanders in a bullying situation.

Some bystanders are allies of the bully. They follow the lead of the bully and join in tormenting the victim. These henchmen don't start the bullying themselves, but they act as backup and take direction from the bully. These assistant bullies sometimes band together in their own social group with insiders who look down on the outsiders.

Encouragers act as an appreciative audience although they do not take part in bullying the victim themselves. They might prod the bully to pick on the victim or laugh at the victim's humiliation. They may pretend to approve of the bullying just to guarantee that they don't antagonize the bully and become the next victim.

Disengaged observers don't take sides and try to act indifferent toward the scenario going on before them. They try to ignore the bullying and expect that the situation will be resolved without their involvement. Bullies, however, interpret their neutrality as acceptance or even approval of their actions. And when the victim is surrounded by people who either enjoy the spectacle or act as if they don't care, it makes him or her feel even more isolated.

Potential allies also avoid taking sides, but they're upset by the bullying and feel guilty about standing by without taking action. They may be afraid that the bully will target them next if they speak up, or they lack confidence in themselves, believing that they are powerless to help. Subtle peer pressure is also a factor—after all, nobody else is objecting to the bullying, so why should they act any differently? Potential allies may consider telling a teacher or other adult, but they don't want to be labeled a tattletale, or they don't think that it would do any good.

Then there's a final group: defenders or helpful witnesses. These kids act to intervene or get help. But before discussing the ways to support a friend in a bullying situation, one should examine why so many kids fail to act.

FINDING INCENTIVES TO ACT

It can be difficult to make the decision to intervene in a bullying situation. Most kids have witnessed friends or other peers being bullied and had to wrestle with the dilemma of whether they should stand by or take action.

There are a lot of reasons that bystanders fail to stand up for the victim. As mentioned, sometimes kids fear that they'll become the one the bully targets next. They might also be afraid that if they try to stand up to the bully, they'll just exacerbate the situation and make things

Bullies like to put on a show for an audience, and for many bystanders, it's preferable to tolerate the bullying rather than attract the bully's attention by speaking up.

worse. They might even fear that they themselves will get hurt for drawing attention to themselves, or that they would be stigmatized for speaking out amid a crowd of supporters and neutral observers. Perhaps they fear they could lose friends for taking the victim's side. Some bystanders may think that the situation is just none of their concern. It could even be as simple as not knowing what to do to try to help.

By not acting, bystanders contribute to a hostile environment conducive to bullying. Bystanders have more power than they realize. In general, bystanders contribute to the problem by staying silent. If you have a friend being bullied, you're hurting him or her by standing by, even if

THE REASONS VICTIMS DON'T TELL

You might think that if you have a friend who's being bullied, he or she would tell an adult if things started to get really bad. But the truth is that victims often remain silent even if the bullying is making them miserable.

There are many reasons that victims don't tell. They may feel that being bullied means that they're weak, and they're ashamed to admit it to others. They may be afraid that the bully will retaliate, or that other kids will reject them for being a tattletale. They may even think that they deserve the bullying because of their own shortcomings. Also, recall that victims may develop "learned helplessness." They may believe that they can't do anything to help themselves, that adults won't be able to do anything either and, perhaps, that they won't even try.

A victim might subscribe to the myth that bullying is a normal part of growing up, as well, and believe that he or she has no choice but to endure the torment. This isn't true—bullying is a serious problem. It doesn't "toughen kids up," and it can cause emotional scars that can persist long after the victim and bully have parted ways.

you don't think there's any way you can help. When you see a friend being bullied, you can either take direct action or tell an adult about what's happening.

It might not be easy to decide to be a bullying victim's defender, but even receiving support after the incident can help a friend who is being bullied cope.

If you decide to step in or speak up, make sure beforehand that you're in no danger of getting hurt as a result. If that's a possibility, leave the scene and tell an adult instead.

There are many ways you can intervene in a bullying situation. You can simply tell the bully to stop. Other kids who were afraid to speak up may join you. You can create a distraction to draw attention from the bullying. Another possibility is trying to help the victim away from the scene, perhaps by inviting him or her to join another activity or by saying that the teacher wants to talk to him or her. Whatever you do, don't resort to violence.

If you would prefer to avoid drawing attention to yourself, there are also ways that you can support your friend without directly confronting the bully. After the incident is over, you can talk to him or her personally or send a text expressing support. Tell your friend that you're on his or her side and that you're there if your friend would like to talk. A bullying victim will cope much better with a supportive friend—be sure to include your friend in activities and invitations.

In addition, you can try talking to the bully afterward, because he or she may be more willing to listen in private rather than in front of a crowd. Tell the bully that you're not happy with how he or she has been treating your friend. Try to present your reasons without being accusatory so that you can discuss the situation calmly rather than exchange insults.

You can't solve your friend's problems on your own, however. One of the most important actions you can take is to encourage him or her to get help from parents, school administrators, and mental health professionals who are experienced in guiding victims of bullying.

CHAPTER FIVE

SEEKING SUPPORT

Y ou can help a bullied friend a lot just by continuing to extend your friendship. In 2012, the critically acclaimed documentary *BULLY* played in theaters across the country. The movie profiled victims of bullying and dispelled the idea that bullying is just a rite of passage that's no big deal. A companion book by the same name pointed out the importance of having the support of a friend: "Kids who have even one friend to confide in can deal with bullying better than those on their own."

Maybe your friend is grateful to have a friend willing to listen about his or her troubles. On the other hand, it could be that your friend is reluctant to discuss the bullying he or she is experiencing. It could be that your friend believes that you would think less of him or her if you knew about how much the bullying

The movie *BULLY* profiled the stories of real-life kids and teens who battled bullying. Alex, a boy with Asperger's syndrome, experienced years of victimization.

was affecting them. Or your friend is convinced that nothing can be done to make things better, so talking about the painful subject won't do anything more than bring up unpleasant associations.

If you're concerned about the effects that bullying is having on your friend, try to bring up the subject tactfully to help him or her open up. Instead of asking directly if a certain person has been bullying him or her, for example, try mentioning that the individual sometimes treats other kids badly.

Remember that your friend doesn't want pity—he or she wants your support and friendship. Assure your friend that you're not going to abandon him or her because of the bullying. Treat your friend with respect. If you're discussing approaches to stop the bullying, don't try to impose your opinions on your friend without considering his or her views. The bullying may have left your friend feeling powerless, and it will benefit him or her to devise a strategy and put it into action. Emphasize to your friend that he or she isn't helpless and has options to deal with the bullying.

One thing is certain: you should urge your friend to talk with an adult about the problem. Kids sometimes make the mistake of thinking that there's nothing adults can do—that they don't really understand kids' lives at school and would just make things worse by intervening. In reality, adults have the authority, knowledge, and experience for dealing with bullying situations.

YOUR ADULT ALLIES

Your friend may be unwilling to inform adults about the

bullying he or she is experiencing. One reason may be fear that your friend will be labeled a "tattletale" and shunned. Reassure your friend that there's a difference between tattling and telling. Kids tattle for petty reasons—to get someone else into trouble, perhaps, or to get attention. When there is a genuine problem that needs to be rectified, or if someone's well-being is in danger, informing an adult qualifies as telling or reporting the problem. Bullying is a situation that requires action by the adults responsible for keeping kids safe.

Parents can help your friend take steps to "bully-proof" themselves. Learning that their son or daughter has been a bullying victim can be an incentive to spend more quality time together and to listen and respond to his or her concerns. They can offer encouragement to their son or daughter to improve his or her self-esteem, confidence, and social skills. They can also help a child work out strategies for handling situations that might lead to bullying. Parents can arrange activities that can provide an antidote to the bullying and provide a chance to form social relationships, whether it's something small like having friends over or a larger commitment such as signing up for martial arts classes. Parents can also contact school personnel, mental health professionals, other parents, and, if necessary, law enforcement.

Teachers and school personnel can implement antibullying policies that promote a healthy learning environment and support individual victims of bullying. Teachers can intervene and shut down a bullying situation. Ideally, they know the children involved and will be able to determine whether a bully has been targeting a specific victim. They can take practical measures to prevent further bullying, such as putting together a new seating chart or keeping an eye on the victim during less structured activities. Teachers and school administrators will also take action about the bully. Your friend shouldn't be discouraged if the bully isn't disciplined severely, however. Some schools try to intervene with bullies and try to change their behavior rather than punish them. They may be required to write a letter of apology or perform a good deed for the victim or the school. If the bully persists in targeting others, however, the consequences will be more severe.

Your friend's parents or teacher may recommend that he or she see a school counselor, psychologist, or other mental health professional. Your friend may be reluctant to consent because of the stigma sometimes associated with

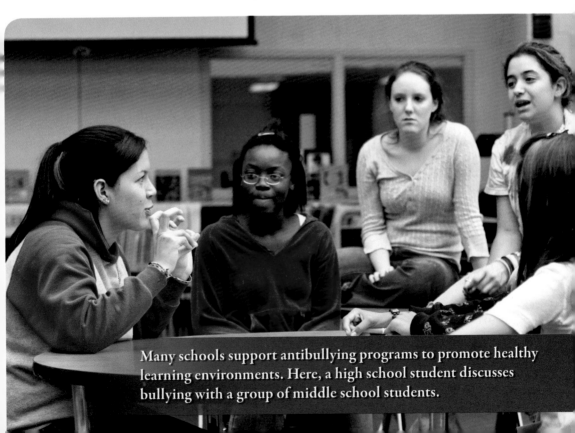

Many schools support antibullying programs to promote healthy learning environments. Here, a high school student discusses bullying with a group of middle school students.

WHEN THE BULLY IS THE TEACHER

The prevalence of bullying in schools has been widely discussed, but many people are unaware that teachers can be bullies, too. In one notorious 2011 incident, a Tennessee teacher taunted a kindergarten student for his messy work area and encouraged the other students to "oink" at him. According to WebMD, a survey of teachers found that 45 percent admitted to bullying a student. Some target a specific individual for unfair criticism. Others belittle students who ask questions about lessons, telling them that they are stupid for not understanding the material.

If you have a friend who is being bullied by a teacher, urge your friend to tell his or her parents about the situation. They can take actions such as talking with the teacher, contacting administrators, reporting abusive behavior, and documenting communications with the teacher. School officials are sometimes reluctant to challenge a teacher who is bullying a student, however. Your friend will appreciate your support while the situation is being resolved.

mental health issues. Assure your friend that it's completely normal for people to see a therapist when experiencing serious challenges in their lives. A therapist or other professional can help your friend build his or her sense of self, improve social skills, practice assertiveness, learn to resolve conflicts, and deal with feelings of pain and anger, as well as address issues such as depression or anxiety. Your friend will gain the strength to deal more confidently with bullying situations and reach out to form friendships.

Adults can be indispensable allies in surviving bullying, but unfortunately, some adults fail to recognize or address bullying. Parents or teachers may act dismissive when a young person reports bullying. Don't give up, though—the government's official stopbullying.gov site recommends telling a "trusted adult" and that you "Try talking to as many adults as possible if there's a problem—teachers, counselors, custodians, nurses, parents. The more adults they involve, the better."

KNOWING THE LAW

As a victim of bullying, your friend probably has the law on his or her side. Most states have laws and policies intended to combat bullying. There is no national law addressing bullying, but in 2011, President Barack Obama held the first White House Conference on Bullying Prevention. Subsequently, the US Department of Education has released guidelines on bullying policies and issued reports on different approaches.

Today, most states have antibullying laws and antibullying policies that serve as models for districts developing their own rules. The states address bullying through both education law—such as in state education codes—and criminal law, which approaches bullying as a criminal matter. These laws establish procedures for responding to, investigating, and disciplining bullying. Your friend can ask for a copy of your school's

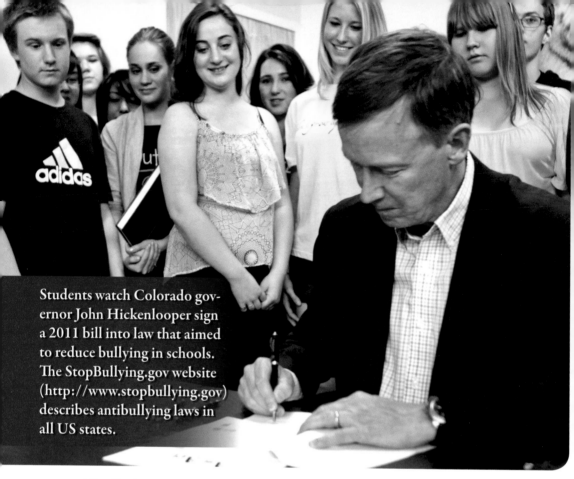

Students watch Colorado governor John Hickenlooper sign a 2011 bill into law that aimed to reduce bullying in schools. The StopBullying.gov website (http://www.stopbullying.gov) describes antibullying laws in all US states.

anti-bullying policy and check the relevant state laws.

Many antibullying procedures allow anonymous reporting to counteract the stigma of "tattling." For example, some schools have hotlines or confidential email reporting systems that guarantee that nobody will find out the identity of the witness.

Law enforcement is also involved in antibullying policies. Police and other law enforcement personnel participate in bullying prevention initiatives, educate the community on state antibullying laws and policies, supervise problematic locations and events, investigate bullying incidents, and meet with students and parents. If the bullying involved a crime, such as assault or a hate crime, the bully could face criminal charges.

CHAPTER SIX

STRATEGIES AND RESOURCES

I t's easy for the victim of a bully to feel isolated, helpless, and hopeless. You can help your friend realize that he or she is not alone and that you can both take steps to boost your friend's confidence in dealing with bullying. There are many guides and supportive websites available to help deal with bullying and the aftermath. Your friend can survey some of these resources and learn what advice works best for him or her. There's no single proven solution that can make everything better, but with persistence and confidence, your friend will find effective help and become happy and healthy once again.

GET THE INFO

Bullying victims can be worn down by the bully's torment until they feel that there's nothing they can do to help themselves. You should encourage your friend to take advantage of resources that can help him or her understand and thwart bullying. Stop by your school or public library and check out books about bullying that can provide you with information

Young people who are bullied sometimes have trouble fitting in with the crowd. You can help your friend recognize his own talents and strengths and develop confidence in dealing with peers.

and guidance. Many are told from a teen's point of view. They also provide contacts for organizations and lists of websites. Memoirs and other personal accounts describe how other people survived being bullied, and plenty of novels address bullying, as well.

Your friend can consult the internet for reputable websites that educate about bullying and offer tips for dealing with bullies. Sites provide a wealth of information as well as antibullying advocacy opportunities.

Do not forget about the resources readily available at your school. Your friend can request a copy of your school's antibullying policy and ask about any antibullying programs offered.

You can also talk over strategies for dealing with bullies with your friend. Books and websites provide a great deal of general information, and discussing it can help your friend determine what approaches are most effective for him or her. For example, some of the typical settings for bullying are hallways, classrooms before lessons, locker rooms, buses, and the cafeteria. In which places does your friend most fear bullying? Experts generally advise that bullying victims act assertive, but avoid fighting back. What approach would work the best with the person or group targeting your friend? Try out role-playing scenarios with your friend so that he or she can practice possible responses to a bully.

Don't treat your friend as if you think he or she is fragile. Your friend doesn't want delicate treatment—he or she just wants life to be normal. Also, your friend shouldn't try to change who he or she is as a response to bullying. Kids shouldn't be ashamed of being themselves. But your friend can develop new strengths and tactics to deal with bullying.

GETTING ON WITH LIFE

Bullying doesn't define your friend, but bullying can cause your friend to retreat inward and lose interest in favorite activities. If your friend has been severely affected by bullying, urge him or her to make a purposeful effort to reach out and rebuild a healthy lifestyle. Experts sometimes refer to this as a healing process. Ideally, school personnel and teachers will work to resolve the bullying situation affecting your friend, and he or she will be able to draw on the support of parents as well as the guidance offered by a counselor or therapist. But these people can't fix your friend's well-being any more than you can do so. Your friend needs to resolve it to make the most of life despite bullying.

Bullying victims often take up practices that can help build confidence, overcome negative thoughts, and deal with stress. Examples include journaling, exercise, meditation, and positive self-talk. This means, for example, that when your friend starts to get nervous before entering a classroom where he or she has been bullied, your friend will tell him or herself, "I can manage this, and I'm going to do my best in class today."

Extracurricular activities, hobbies, and other pursuits will give your friend a chance to make and sustain friendships as well as participate in new interests. Examples include school clubs, electives such as art classes at a community center, music lessons, or student government. Perhaps your friend can look into specific interests—LGBT teens might consider an LGBT youth group or gay-straight alliance; a kid tormented for being a nerd might join a science club. Some bullying victims take up martial arts, not for self-defense but because of the self-confidence it imparts. Kids who have been bullied often benefit from activities that help others, as well, such as working with a community organization or walking dogs for a local animal shelter.

You and your friends could also get involved in antibullying programs at your school. If you discover that the antibullying policies and resources are ineffective,

Many bullying victims find that writing down their feelings can help them cope with the experience. Writing poetry or stories can also offer a means of release.

AMANDA TODD'S LEGACY

Sadly, antibullying reforms are sometimes spurred by tragedy. On September 7, 2012, Amanda Todd, a fifteen-year-old Canadian student with a learning disability, posted a video titled "Amanda Todd: Struggling, Bullying, Suicide, Self Harm, Fighting" in which she held up a series of flashcards showing her handwritten story. She had been targeted online by a pedophile in seventh grade. He had persuaded her to post a topless photo of herself, and, later, he asked for her to "put on a show" for him. When she refused, he sent the photos to her family and friends. Instead of supporting her, her classmates taunted and physically bullied her. The internet stalking and bullying by her peers followed her as she switched schools multiple times. Amanda began suffering from depression and anxiety, and she resorted to substance abuse and self-harm. A month after posting her video, she killed herself. After widespread publicity over the incident, legislators introduced antibullying measures in the Canadian parliament.

Other high-profile suicides linked to bullying have also led to outcry and action. After thirteen-year-old Ryan Halligan experienced cyberbullying and killed himself in 2003, Vermont enacted a Bully Prevention Law. In 2006, thirteen-year-old Megan Meier killed herself after being deceived and tormented online, prompting Missouri's "Megan's Law" criminalizing cyberbullying.

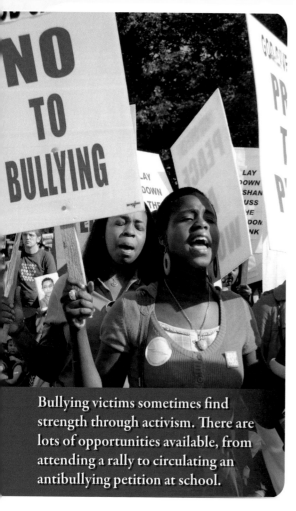

Bullying victims sometimes find strength through activism. There are lots of opportunities available, from attending a rally to circulating an antibullying petition at school.

you could take steps to draw awareness to the issue. You could urge the school to adopt an antibullying pledge, for example. Other possible ideas include introducing measures to track incidents of bullying, offering peer counseling, or screening and discussing the documentary *BULLY*.

CHAPTER SEVEN

LESSONS FOR LIFE

Incidences of bullying tend to decrease at higher school grades—young children are much more likely to experience bullying than high school upperclassmen. The time will come when your friend is free of school bullying and can leave that painful stage of life behind. Nevertheless, bullying is essentially an abuse of power, and it's possible that you or your friend may encounter bullies further on in life.

MOVING ON

Being a victim of bullying is a traumatic experience. As described earlier, many adults retain emotional scars from childhood bullying. If it is not addressed, bullying can have a long-term impact on personal life choices and career trajectories. But as the "It Gets Better" project emphasizes, the bullying will eventually end and life will indeed get better in the future, particularly if supportive adults and loyal friends help the bullying victim throughout the experience.

SEXUAL HARASSMENT OR BULLYING?

If your friend has been targeted by unwanted, malicious behavior from peers, is it a case of bullying or is it actually harassment? Although the two situations tend to overlap, the definition of harassment is narrower. According to stopbullying.gov, "harassment is unwelcome conduct based on a protected class (race, national origin, color, sex, age, disability, religion) that is severe, pervasive, or persistent and creates a hostile environment." If a bully targets your friend, it's bullying, but if a bully picks on your friend because of his or her race, gender, or other status, it's also harassment. Victims of harassment have recourse to a variety of federal and state laws.

Sexual harassment—sometimes also called "gendered bullying"—is unwelcome behavior based on gender and sexual orientation. Unwanted touching can qualify as physical harassment; unwanted sexual comments or advances can be considered verbal harassment. Homophobic insults can also count as sexual harassment, and both males and females can be victims of sexual harassment. Cyberbullying can involve sexual harassment, as well.

Sexual harassment is often overlooked in schools. Peers and even teachers may think that it's just flirting or categorize aggressive attention as bullying rather than harassment. As with bullying, victims of sexual harassment are sometimes reluctant to come forward.

Individuals who do report an incident to their school have recourse to federal laws protecting against sexual harassment.

Still, memories of the bullying will occasionally arise. An aggressive confrontation might suddenly remind the former victim of childhood bullying. There's nothing unusual about such incidents. When it happens, your friend should just remember that he or she is not a victim anymore and that bullies in any context don't have any control over him or her.

Some former victims even gain a sense of personal empowerment from their success in overcoming the experience of being bullied. These individuals learn about their own strengths and the value of getting up and trying again after facing adversity. They are able to claim to have a strong sense of self because their belief in themselves has been tested. Chances are, they also came to appreciate the value of true friendship and of the help offered by others while getting their lives back on track.

BULLYING IN THE ADULT WORLD

Bullying doesn't necessarily stop after you're out of school. Bullying can be an issue for adults, as well. It can occur within families and among neighborhoods and communities. It can happen online, as well—adults can be cyberbullies. When Megan Meier was bullied online, one of the villains was the mother of a peer.

Adult bullying is not widely addressed, but the form that generates the most discussion is workplace bullying. Workplace bullying is similar to school bullying in many ways. It involves an imbalance of power between the bully and victim and the bullying is repeated over time. Kids are torn between working to succeed in school and giving up because of the pain of bullying; adults do their best to perform their job even as bullying makes the experience miserable. Workplace bullying can damage the victim's emotional health and career prospects. It also contributes to a hostile work atmosphere and costs employers financially in terms of absenteeism and reduced performance by bullied workers.

A 2010 survey cited by *SFGate* found that 35 percent of workers have been bullied at work. The bully in the workplace is often the boss. Instead of providing leadership, a bully boss may create a toxic work environment. The bullying can be obvious, such as unfair criticism or insults, or it can be more covert, such as cutting off communication or sabotaging projects. Co-workers can be bullies, too, and may target a victim by spreading rumors or excluding him or her from job-related social events. Many adult bullies were formerly bullies, or even bully-victims, at school.

As with playground bullying, adult victims of workplace bullying sometimes don't realize that they're being bullied. The bullying is usually verbal or relational, and adults can be more subtle than kids. When victims recognize the behavior as bullying, they sometimes don't know what to do or may be unwilling to risk their jobs by complaining. An adult being bullied in the workplace should document instances of bullying and report it to a manager or human

Workplace bullying is a pattern of abusive behaviors that can lead to health consequences for the victim and contribute to a stressful work environment for all employees.

resources department. When the manager is the bully, however, the situation is more difficult to resolve.

If you're a former bullying victim, or if you helped a friend take a stand against bullying, you're well equipped for dealing with an adult bully. You'll be able to recognize the situation and refuse to play the part of a beaten-down victim. You will be familiar with procedures for reporting bullying and recourses for recovering from the consequences of the experience. Workplaces, like schools, can benefit from awareness of bullying and a refusal to let bullying take a toll.

GLOSSARY

AGGRESSIVE Acting in a confrontational or overly forceful manner.

ALLY A supporter; a person or organization willing to help or cooperate with another.

ANXIETY An emotion characterized by feelings of tension, worried thoughts, and physical changes like increased blood pressure.

ASSERTIVE Acting in a confident and self-assured manner.

BULLYING Unwanted, aggressive behavior among school-aged children that involves a real or perceived power imbalance. The behavior is repeated, or has the potential to be repeated, over time.

BYSTANDER A peer who witnesses bullying.

CONSEQUENCE A result or outcome of some previous occurrence.

CYBERBULLYING Bullying that takes place using electronic technology, including devices and equipment such as cell phones, computers, and tablets, as well as communication tools such as social media sites, text messages, instant messaging, and websites.

DEPRESSION A mental illness in which feelings of sadness, loss, anger, or frustration interfere with everyday life for an extended period of time.

FRUSTRATION A feeling of annoyance or dissatisfaction, especially because of unresolved problems or an inability to accomplish something.

GUIDANCE Advice or help, especially from someone in a position of expertise or authority.

HARASSMENT Unwelcome conduct based on a protected class (race, national origin, color, sex, age, disability, religion) that is severe, pervasive, or persistent and creates a hostile environment.

INTERVENE To come between parties involved in a dispute to mediate or help settle it.

NEUTRAL Not taking sides in a dispute.

OBSERVER Someone watching what is going on.

PEDOPHILE An adult who is sexually attracted to young children.

POLICY A course of action adopted by a government, business, or other group.

RELATIONAL BULLYING Bullying that targets someone's reputation or relationships.

SUICIDE The act of intentionally taking one's life.

VICTIM Someone who is hurt or who has suffered as a result of another person's actions.

FOR MORE INFORMATION

Boys Town
National Headquarters
  14100 Crawford Street
  Boys Town, NE 68010
  (402) 498-1300
  Hotline: (800) 448-3000
  Website: http://www.boystown.org
  Boys Town works to give at-risk children and families the
  love, support, and education they need to succeed. In addition,
  the Boys Town National Hotline has helped millions of teens,
  parents, and families on the brink of disaster.

BullyingCanada
  471 Smythe Street
  PO BOX 27009
  Fredericton, NB E3B 9M1
  Canada
  (877) 352-4497
  Website: https://www.bullyingcanada.ca
  BullyingCanada offers information, help, and support to
  everyone involved in bullying—the victim, perpetrator,
  bystander, parents, school staff, and the community at large.

The BULLY Project
  18 West 27th Street, 2nd Floor
  New York, NY 10001
  (212) 725-1220
  Website: http://www.thebullyproject.com
  The BULLY Project is the social action campaign inspired by
  the award-winning film *BULLY*.

Crisis Call Center
  PO Box 8016
  Reno, NV 89507
  (775) 784-8085
  Hotline: (800) 273-8255
  Website: http://www.crisiscallcenter.org
  Crisis Call Center's twenty-four-hour crisis line often serves as the first point of contact for individuals who are seeking help, support, and information.

It Gets Better Project
  110 South Fairfax Avenue, Suite A11-71
  Los Angeles, CA 90036
  Website: http://www.itgetsbetter.org
  The It Gets Better Project works to communicate to lesbian, gay, bisexual, and transgender youth around the world that it gets better, and it offers a message of hope. It encourages change and inspires people to stop harassment and bullying around the world.

Kids Help Phone
  300-439 University Avenue
  Toronto, ON M5G 1Y8
  Canada
  (416) 586-5437
  Hotline: (800) 668-6868
  Website: http://www.kidshelpphone.ca
  Kids Help Phone is Canada's only 24/7 counseling and information service for young people who are ages twenty and under. The professionally-trained counselors provide a service that is anonymous, confidential, and nonjudgmental.

WEBSITES

Because of the changing nature of internet links, Rosen Publishing has developed an online list of websites related to the subject of this book. This site is updated regularly. Please use this link to access the list:

http://www.rosenlinks.com/HCIH/bully

FOR FURTHER READING

Blume, Judy. *Blubber*. New York, NY: Atheneum Books for Young Readers, 2014.

Hanson-Harding, Alexandra. *How to Beat Physical Bullying* (Beating Bullying). New York, NY: Rosen Publishing, 2013.

Landau, Jennifer. *Dealing with Bullies, Cliques, and Social Stress* (The Middle School Survival Handbook). New York, NY: Rosen Publishing, 2013.

Landau, Jennifer. *How to Beat Psychological Bullying* (Beating Bullying). New York, NY: Rosen Publishing, 2013.

Langan, Paul. *Bullying in Schools: What You Need to Know*. West Berlin, NJ: Townsend Press, 2011.

Lohmann, Raychelle Cassada, and Julia V. Taylor. *The Bullying Workbook for Teens: Activities to Help You Deal with Social Aggression and Cyberbullying*. Oakland, CA: Instant Help Books, 2013.

Manrock, Aija. *The Survival Guide to Bullying: Written by a Teen*. New York, NY: Scholastic, 2015.

Medina, Meg. *Yaqui Delgado Wants to Kick your Ass*. Somerville, MA: Candlewick Press, 2013.

Metcalf, Dawn. *Dear Bully: Seventy Authors Tell Their Stories*. New York, NY: HarperTeen, 2011.

Meyer, Stephanie, et al. *Bullying Under Attack: True Stories Written by Teen Victims, Bullies and Bystanders*. Deerfield Beach, FL: Health Communications, 2013.

Porterfield, Jason. *How to Beat Social Alienation* (Beating Bullying). New York, NY: Rosen Publishing, 2013.

Scherer, Lauri S. *Cyberbullying*. Farmington Hills, MI: Greenhaven Press, 2015.

Sonneborn, Liz. *How to Beat Verbal Bullying* (Beating Bullying). New York, NY: Rosen Publishing, 2013.

BIBLIOGRAPHY

Brown, Kristen V. "Workplace Bullying More Common than Most Think." *SFGate*, November 6, 2013 (http://www.sfgate.com/health/article/Workplace-bullying-more-common-than-most-think-4958484.php).

Carpenter, Deborah, and Cristopher J. Ferguson. *The Everything Parent's Guide to Dealing with Bullies*. Avon, MA: Adams Media, 2009.

Coloroso, Barbara. *The Bully, the Bullied, and the Bystander*. New York, HY: HarperCollins, 2008.

Dombeck, Mark. "The Long Term Effects of Bullying." MentalHelp.net, July 24, 2007 (https://www.mentalhelp.net/articles/the-long-term-effects-of-bullying/).

Fowler, Bob. "Kindergarten Teacher Has Kids Oink at Student Who Was Messy." *Knoxville News Sentinel*, April 13, 2011 (http://www.knoxnews.com/news/local/kindergarten-teacher-has-kids-oink-at-student-who-was-messy-ep-405060263-357926321.html).

Goldman, Carrie. *Bullied: What Every Parent, Teacher and Kid Need to Know about Ending the Cycle of Fear*. New York, NY: HarperCollins, 2012.

Hirsch, Lee, Cynthia Lowen, and Dina Santorelli, eds. *Bully: An Action Plan for Teachers, Parents, and Communities to Combat the Bullying Crisis*. New York, NY: Weinstein Books, 2012.

Kam, Katherine. "Teachers Who Bully." *WebMD*, 2016 (http://www.webmd.com/parenting/features/teachers-who-bully).

Kuykendall, Sally. *Bullying*. Santa Barbara, CA: Greenwood, 2012.

Middelton-Moz, Jane, and Mary Lee Zawadski. *Bullies: Strategies for Survival*. Deerfield Beach, FL: Health Communications, 2002.

Pappas, Stephanie. "The Pain of Bullying Lasts into Adulthood." *LiveScience*, February 20, 2013. (http://www.livescience.com/27279-bullying-effects-last-adulthood.html).

"Prevent Bullying." StopBullying.gov, 2016 (http://www.stopbullying.gov/prevention/index.html).

Robers, Simone, Arlan Zhang, Rachel E. Morgan, and Lauren Musu-Gillette. "Indicators of School Crime and Safety: 2014." US Department of Education, 2015 (http://nces.ed.gov/pubs2015/2015072.pdf).

Savage, Dan, and Terry Miller, eds. *It Gets Better: Coming Out, Overcoming Bullying, and Creating a Life Worth Living*. New York, NY: Dutton, 2011.

Steele, Ann. "The Psychological Effects of Bullying on Kids & Teens." MasterInPsychologyGuide.com, 2016 (http://mastersinpsychologyguide.com/articles/psychological-effects-bullying-kids-teens).

Strauss, Susan L. *Sexual Harassment and Bullying: A Guide to Keeping Kids Safe and Holding Schools Accountable*. Lanham, MD: Rowman & Littlefield Publishers, Inc., 2012.

Subramanian, Mathangi. *Bullying: It Happened to Me*. Lanham, MD: Rowman & Littlefield, 2014.

Szalavitz, Maia. "The Tragic Case of Amanda Todd." *Time*, October 16, 2012 (http://healthland.time.com/2012/10/16/the-tragic-case-of-amanda-todd/).

INDEX

ABOUT THE AUTHOR

Corona Brezina has written numerous books for young adults. Several of her previous works have focused on health and legal issues concerning teens, including *Being a Foster Child* and *Alcohol and Drug Offenses: Your Legal Rights*. She lives in Chicago, Illinois.

PHOTO CREDITS